EXPOSED:

THE TACTICS OF THE ENEMY
NO ONE IS TALKING ABOUT

EXPOSED: THE TACTICS OF THE ENEMY NO ONE IS TALKING ABOUT
Copyright © 2019 by Decisions Determine Destiny Press

All rights reserved. No part of this publication may be reproduced, distributed, or transmitted in any form or by any means, including photocopying, recording, or other electronic or mechanical methods, without the prior written permission of the publisher, except in the case of brief quotations embodied in critical reviews and certain other noncommercial uses permitted by copyright law. For permission requests, write to the publisher, addressed "Attention: Permissions Coordinator," at the address below. Scripture quotations from The Authorized (King James) Version. Rights in the Authorized Version in the United Kingdom are vested in the Crown. Reproduced by permission of the Crown's patentee, Cambridge University Press

ISBN: 98 09927 831 74 (Paperback)
ISBN: 978-0-000000-0 (Hardcover)

Any references to historical events, real people, or real places are used fictitiously.
Orders by U.K. trade bookstores and wholesalers. Please Decisions Determine Destiny Press
Email: info@decisionsdeterminedestiny.com
Website: www.kevintreasure.com

Book cover design by: Spiffing Covers
Printed by Decisions Determine Destiny Press

First printing edition 2019.

Copyright © 2019
All rights reserved
Printed in the United States
Printed in the United Kingdom
First Edition 2019

EXPOSED:

THE TACTICS OF THE ENEMY NO ONE IS TALKING ABOUT

Therefore rejoice, you heavens, and you that dwell in them. Woe to the inhabitants of the earth and of the sea, for the devil has come down unto you, having great wrath, because he knows that he has but a short time.

Revelation 12:12

Be sober, be vigilant; because your adversary the devil walks about like a roaring lion, seeking whom he may devour.

1st Peter 5:8

Table of Contents

AUTHOR'S NOTE I
WE ARE AT WAR….. III
1 - THE ASSIGNMENT AGAINST:THE SINGLE WOMEN 1
2 - ENTICE THE CHURCH TO JUMP ON EVERYTHING THAT THE WORLD SYSTEM IS DOING.. 3
3 - OUTSIDE INFLUENCE:SEND IN THE WOLVES 4
4 - CAUSE THE CHRISTIAN TO ACT LIKE THE WORLD 5
5 - TELL PEOPLE ONLY THE BAD THINGS THAT HAPPEN IN THE CHURCH 6
6 - PROMOTE HYPOCRISY 7
7 - ENTICE THE CHRISTIAN TO WALK IN THE FLESH 8
8 - PROMOTE STRIFE 9
9 - USE CONTENTIOUS PEOPLE TO SOW DISCORD 10
10 - DOCTRINAL DIFFERENCES 11
11 - GIVE THEM A DESIRE FOR THE SUPERNATURAL BUT NO DESIRE TO LEARN THE BIBLE 12
12 - PROMOTE THE NOVICE QUICKLY 13
13 - PROMOTE RELIGION AND LEGALISM OVER PERSONAL RELATIONSHIP 14
14 - NO VISION 16
15 - PUFF THE GIFTED ONES(AN OLD FAVOURITE) 18
16 - OFFER THE GIFTED ONES THE WORLD.................................... 19
17 - PROMOTE A PEOPLE FRIENDLY GOSPEL 20

18 - PROMOTE A BLESS ME GOSPEL 21
19 - THE PROMOTION OF HOMOSEXUALITY AND PERSECUTION OF THE CHURCH 22
20 - INFLUENCE THE CHRISTIAN TO WORK OUTSIDE THE TIMING OF GOD 24
21 - PROMOTE COMPETITION AMONGST MINISTERS 25
22 - GLAMORIZE A PARTICULAR MINISTRY OVER ANOTHER 27
23 - USE MINISTERS TO ATTACK OTHER MINISTERS 28
24 - FRUSTRATION 29
25 - PLACE THE WRONG PERSON OVER THE FINANCES 30
26 - USE STRONG FINANCIAL MEMBERS TO CONTROL THE LEADER 31
27 - CHARACTER ASSASSINATION 32
28 - CAUSE THEM TO BLAME GOD FOR THE BAD THINGS THAT HAPPEN 33
29 - REMINDERS OF THE PAST 35
30 - DISCOURAGE THE WORKERS 36
31 - DISTRACTION 37
32 - DISGRUNTLED EX-MEMBERS 38
33 - MISERABLE DOOR STAFF 39
34 - BAGGAGE FROM THEIR LAST MINISTRY 40
35 - PROMOTE THE ANOINTING AND WISDOM IMBALANCE IN THE CHURCH 41
36 - CAUSE THE CHURCH TO MAJOR ON THE MINORS 43
37 - MAKE THE CHURCH LOOK OUT OF TOUCH 44

38 - ISOLATE THE LEADER 45

39 - PROMOTE FALSE CONVERSIONS 46

40 - PRIDE 47

41 - NEVER CAUSE THE BACKSLIDER TO RETURN 49

42 - JEZEBEL: THE MASTER MANIPULATOR 50

43 - ABSALOM: THE HEART STEALER 52

44 - THEY MUST NEVER BE ALLOWED TO RECOGNIZE THEIR AUTHORITY AS BELIEVERS 53

45 - FIGHT AGAINST THE MINISTRIES WHICH DEMONSTRATE HEALING AND DELIVERANCE 54

46 - THEY MUST NEVER BE ALLOWED TO RECOGNIZE THE POWER OF PRAISE AND WORSHIP 55

47 - IF THEY GET SAVED, THEY MUST NEVER RENEW THEIR MIND .. 56

48 - PROMOTE REPLACEMENT THEORY 57

49 - PROMOTE RACISM 58

50 - USE THE ABUSE COMMITTED BY SOME MINISTERS TO DISCREDIT THEIR BELIEF 59

51 - ATTACK THE MIND 60

52 - MAKE MINISTRY LOOK EASY 62

53 - MAKE SEX NON-EXISTENT IN THE MARRIAGE OF MINISTERS 63

54 - THE SPEAR OF SAUL 64

55 - USE THE WEAPON OF OFFENCE TO KEEP THEM DIVIDED 66

56 - UNFORGIVENESS: HELL'S GREATEST WEAPON 67

57 - THE LURE OF PORNOGRAPHY 68

58 - USE GOSSIP TO DESTROY THE CHURCH 70

59 - THE ASSIGNMENT AGAINST:THE PRAISE AND WORSHIP TEAM . 72

60 - THE ASSIGNMENT AGAINST: THE PROPHETIC 74

61 - DISCREDIT THE PROPHETIC 76

62 - THE ASSIGNMENT AGAINST MARRIAGE: ADULTERY 78

63 - THE ASSIGNMENT AGAINST:THE TEENAGERS 80

64 - THE ASSIGNMENT AGAINSTTHEIR FINANCES: KEEP THEM BROKE 82

65 - KEEP THEM FROM TITHING AND GIVING 83

66 - GIVE THEM A STINGY SPIRIT 84

67 - THE ASSIGNMENT AGAINST EVANGELISM:DISCOURAGE EVANGELISM 85

68 - THE ASSIGNMENT AGAINST:THE PASTOR'S WIFE...................... 86

69 - THE ASSIGNMENT AGAINST:THE PASTOR 88

70 - WORK THE PASTOR TO DEATH 89

71 - THE LEADER THAT WILL LISTEN TO NO ONE 90

72 - PHYSICAL EXERCISE MUST BE ALIEN TO THE LEADER 91

73 - GET THE PASTOR ANGRY...CONTINUALLY 92

74 - BURNOUT THE PASTOR 94

75 - DISCOURAGEMENT THROUGH UNGRATEFULNESS 95

76 - CREATE A MAN-CENTERED LEADERSHIP 96

77 - DETER THE PASTOR FROM PREACHINGTHE RETURN OF CHRIST 97

78 - THE MINISTER MUST NOT SPEND TIME WITH GOD 98

79 - PROMOTE REBELLION TOWARDS LEADERSHIP 99

80 - GO TO WORK ON THE FLAW IN THE MAN OR WOMAN OF GOD 100

81 - GIVE THE MINISTER A PROBLEM SO EMBARRASSING HE CANNOT BRING IT TO ANYONE 101

82 - LET THE MINISTER SAVE EVERYONE ELSE'S FAMILY EXCEPT THEIR OWN 102

83 - INFLUENCE THE PASTOR TO BUILD WITHOUT GOD 103

84 - GIVE THE PASTOR A DESIRE TO BE FAMOUS 105

85 - DISCREDIT THE LEADER 106

86 - MONEY MUST BE THE NEW MOTIVATION OF THE PREACHER AND NOT THE GOSPEL 107

87 - THE MINISTRY TEAM 108

88 - THE LEADER MUST NEVER RECOGNISE THOSE SENT INTO THEIR LIFE TO AID THEM IN THEIR LIFE ASSIGNMENT 109

90 - WHATEVER YOU DO, DON'T LET THEM…..SEEK FOR THE BAPTISM OF THE HOLY SPIRIT 112

91 - WHATEVER YOU DO, DON'T LET THEM…..BUILD UP THEIR FAITH 114

92 - OUR NUMBER ONE AIM:THE SINNER MUST NEVER GET SAVED 115

WANT TO KNOW GOD? 116

AUTHOR'S NOTE

First, I give honour to my Lord and Saviour, Jesus Christ of Nazareth! Thank you for your Grace that I did not deserve and your unfailing love towards me! Truly the God we serve is a good God, and I am eternally grateful for all he has done. As a writer of several books, 'Exposed: The Tactics of the Enemy No One is Talking About' is by far the most controversial one I have written to date.

The book you are holding in your hand is a by-product of many years of observation of the enemy's schemes, plans and attacks on people's lives as well as his subtle influence toward the believer to, deceive, lie, separate, divide and conquer God's set apart people. He is the father of lies, and his best weapon is deception which he has used and continues to use in the world today.

Many of the tactics mentioned in the book will be deemed controversial and may at times be offensive to some. However, these are real issues being side-lined in the body of Christ today. The viewpoint from which this book has been written will be questioned by many, but the choice was made to write this book from the standpoint of our enemy. When we Christians realize the traps and sometimes hidden (and sometimes visible) snares laid out for them, I believe we will become more vigilant and less blind to the enemy's schemes.

I believe it's time to face the things that no one wants to discuss and stop being ignorant of the things that are taking place. Our churches, leaders, marriages, children, and families are under attack, but God has given us power through his Son Christ Jesus against all the powers of the enemy. When we know who we are and whose we are, we will see the battle is already won! God has given us, his people the person of the Holy Spirit who is with us and upon us. He will not leave us orphans. Prayer and the word are our weapons against the enemy. I have not left you, the reader, with controversial tactics planned by the enemy. I have provided the Solution, The Warning and the Counterattack which are all found in the Word of God, the Bible. There are many great Christian books out there, but believer The Bible must be your life. The answers are in the Book.

As you read, ask the Lord to show you areas of your life where you have been ignorant and take affirmative action by applying God's word to your life.

You are an Overcomer!

Kevin Treasure

WE ARE AT WAR...

When you became a Christian, you were automatically enlisted in the battle, but the difference between this war and any other battle that was ever fought is that we already know we have the victory.

'having stripped the principalities and the powers, he made a show of them openly, triumphing over them in it. (Colossians 2:15)

The devil has been defeated, and Jesus put him to open shame, humiliating him. He has lost, but he from the very beginning, has been planning mankind's downfall, starting with Adam where mankind lost their authority and handed it over to Satan. It was won back through Christ's death, resurrection and ascension and the good news is he has given it to us.

But your enemy is resilient. He'll stop at nothing to hinder, derail and prevent you from succeeding. This unseen enemy is out to destroy your mind, health, family, marriage and soul. He hates you with a passion. He plots and schemes day and night to assure that his evil plans will come to pass concerning your life. He has been around a long time. He has studied the movements and patterns of humanity, and is acquainted and well versed with the temptations and desires that could bring about our demise. He is tenacious in bringing about his plans to pass. He is not playing; he is out to destroy and has an assignment for his number one enemy, The Church.

Jesus said *"I will build my church and the gates of hell shall not prevail against it." (Matthew 16:18)*. God's plan for mankind (as demonstrated through Christ Jesus) is ultimately for our good, but anything Jesus has purposed to build will be the very thing the enemy plans to destroy.

The devil hates everything that God loves and has a plan, an assignment and a goal to carry out its destruction. Gladly, it will never work, because Jesus himself said it was finished and has given us the victory! The enemy and his cohorts are relentless in trying to carry out their plan. When we know the enemy's plans, *we won't be "ignorant of the devil's devices" (2nd Corinthians 2:11)*.

When we are aware of his assignment, we can avoid his traps.

Exposed is your church handbook survival guide to the enemy's tactics.

Some of the tactics you will already be aware of, some you may not. Nevertheless, this book will act as a support system of what to watch for and how to stay alert. There are traps being set every day for your family, marriage, ministry and your very life. However, if we can be made aware, we won't fall prey to the snares that have been set.

As you read, ask the Holy Spirit to enlighten your understanding and give you insight into any areas in your life where you have been ignorant of the devil's devices and ask him for wisdom and grace to deal with and overcome any area where you have been losing.

Exposed reveals the enemy's plans, but also gives you the answer. When Jesus walked the earth, in the time of his temptations the enemy came to the Lord Jesus, but for every temptation Jesus used the Word. He spoke nothing but the word of God. Therefore, the answers for every problem you face is the Word. For every tactic and dart, the enemy throws at Gods people; there is a solution and a way out.

Exposed offers to the reader The Warning, The Counter Attack or The Solution for every tactic thrown your way. God's word is the truth! God's word is spirit and life! God's word is quick, powerful, and sharper than any two-edged sword. He watches over his word to perform it, and it will never return void.

When the enemy mounts his attacks against your life, use God's word.

Victory is yours.

The battle is already won.

He has given you the power.

Exercise your Authority.

**Hell does not want you
to read this book.**

YOUR ENEMY WROTE THIS BOOK.

1

THE ASSIGNMENT AGAINST:
The single women

It's the golden oldie, but it still works a treat.

The church is full of women, it's a fact, I have managed to keep the men distracted with football, basketball, baseball, golf, rugby and every other sport that involves a ball, including music, drugs the love for money, fame, are riches are all the tools I have used to distract them.

However, we must continue to work on the minds of the women. There are millions of single women in churches waiting for their Mr. Right. Many may not say it, but they are all thinking it.

Place people around them that will continually pester them with words that will sink into their spirit: When are you getting married? You're not getting any younger; you don't want to be left on the shelf." These constant suggestions are seeds that will work their way into their heart and mind birth a fear of growing old and lonely with no children.

Fear is our best weapon.

It is this fear that will drive them into the desperation of seeking anyone, preferably someone who does not have a relationship with God and does not love God, in fact, knows nothing about God. The woman will select the man from the perspective of looks, figure, and character, (unbeknown to them, the character is a front (act) for the man to get what he wants…her body).

This is the beginning of the female's downfall process; our aim is to mess up the woman's life by marrying the wrong person who will make her life miserable and eventually cause her to step out of her assignment or leave the things of God altogether due to the embarrassment and treatment she has faced.

If the man can get her to fornicate before they get married even better, if found out the shame of this will bring a snare to her walk with God.

If she chooses to marry the wrong man, then we begin to work on all his ugly qualities she never saw before they were married, his womanizing, smoking drinking, gambling, whatever his persuasion is.

Being a woman, she will have a strong belief that he will change. Depending on the strength of her belief and faith in God, he may change, but not before putting her through hell and back.

Our primary goal is to get them to focus on men outside their belief if they can marry a Muslim; even better, he will do his best to convert her.

If he is unsuccessful, you'll create children who are bombarded with two faiths, culminating in a home ruled by confusion.

If we cannot get her to do this allow her to meet a man in church who's pretending to be a Christian but he's really a pretender. This also works. These tactics can only be accomplished by bombarding the woman's thoughts of being lonely and needing a husband as soon as possible.

This tactic has been working for years; it is my crème de la crème for the ladies.

If we can cause the women to lead a double life, this would be even better. They can attend church, preach, evangelize, sing in the choir, usher at the door and work in Sunday school, but if they're living a double life their witness will be ineffective, and they'll be scared to stand against demons.

THE SOLUTION

But because of the temptation to sexual immorality, each man should have his own wife and each woman her own husband.

1st Corinthians 7:2

2

Entice the church to jump on everything that the world system is doing

It's quite easy when you know how, instead of them spending time with God and obtaining his direction, let them spend hours on social media listening to what the world has to say instead of what God is telling them. They'll be imitating the world system in no time.

We must keep the church a few steps behind the world system; if the church doesn't listen to God, the church will always be playing catch up.

If the church ever gets on the cutting edge of what God is doing and adhere to what he is saying, we will find ourselves on the backburner. So, cause them to doublethink and doubt every thought and idea that was designed to propel them and the gospel to new heights.

Many don't realize that God gives people ideas all the time, but if they do nothing with it, nothing will change. Instead cause them to lean to the world's system, which is my system.

This way the church will only serve as a mirror of the world and not the beacon of light it was created to be.

THE COUNTER ATTACK

The world is passing away, and also its lusts;
but the one who does the will of God lives forever.

1st *John 2:17*

3

Outside Influence: Send in the wolves

As a ministry begins to grow it will attract all kinds of people the good, the bad and the ugly, so we bring in wolves disguised as shepherds. A wolf in sheep's clothing is dangerous; a wolf in a shepherd's attire is pending destruction, so we bring in outside influence at leadership level to diminish the influence of the leader.

Familiarity breeds contempt and people always gravitate to someone new. So, bring a fresh face if they're gifted and charismatic, even better.

A fresh voice with plenty of charisma and you will soon have people flocking to them; the people will tell them all the problems in the church. Now use the wolf to befriend the sheep, help them in any way, gain their trust, by demonstrating whatever gifting they have, then sow discord. How?Start with rumours and then develop slander which will eventually lead to all out discord

End result, church destroyed, sheep scattered, Mission accomplished.

THE COUNTER ATTACK

I appeal to you, brothers, to watch out for those who cause divisions and create obstacles contrary to the doctrine that you have been taught; avoid them.

Romans 16:17

4

Cause the Christian to act like the world

Use your influence to cause the Christian to speak, act and even think like the world. Put no difference between the clean and the profane. This will give sinners the sense of acceptance without feeling conviction, which will cause people to still attend church but yet still cleave to their sin, instead of repenting and turning from the sin.

Having a form of godliness but denying the power thereof.

So, people will now live anyhow they please and still feel they can be called a Christian. This deception is bringing millions to hell. Christian's do not know the damage they cause when they act like the world. They cannot let their light shine if they are acting like those in the dark. Now, sanctification becomes a bad word and holiness is offensive.

Christians cannot affect the very thing they are trying to become like.

THE SOLUTION

Do not love the world or anything in the world. If anyone loves the world, the love of the Father is not in him.

1st *John 2:15*

5

Tell people only the bad things that happen in the church

People are healed, marriages are restored, children are saved, the terminally sick are healed, people are delivered, alcoholics are cleaned up, drug addiction is broken, and many great stories and more fill the churches.

But that is not to be the focus, so cause church people to sideline these stories and chose to magnify only the bad things which are happening in the church.

"Guess who's pregnant?" "His wife is backslidden." "That couple has had a divorce" "That Pastor is a thief." "That woman is a Jezebel," "Her son is on drugs," "Her daughter slept with so." Use every negative story they hear and broadcast it, for free.

When people choose to tell people only the bad things in the church they magnify the negative.

Some Christians talk more about what we are doing than what Jesus is doing, and when people magnify the bad, sinners will stay out, if their life is already a mess why would anyone want to join themselves to an organisation that's not doing any better.

So promote only the bad things that happen in church and dumb down the supernatural. My agents in the media are fantastic at carrying this out.

THE SOLUTION

Conduct yourselves with wisdom toward outsiders,
making the most of the opportunity.

Colossians 4:5

6

Promote hypocrisy

When people refuse to live holy and walk contrary to the word and set a bad example this is what the world will see when they look at the church, so we keep pushing the negative image of the church, that they are all a bunch of hypocrites.

You do this by causing Christians to preach what they don't practise.

Let them preach faithfulness, while the preacher is on his third marriage.

Preach holiness while they are practising the opposite. These things destroy the credibility of the church and turn away true seekers, claiming to be light while still living in the dark, Hypocrisy.

Refusing to change although they know God is speaking to them.

Let them hear the word, agree with the word but don't do the word

Hypocrisy is one of the number one reasons people do not attend church.

Let's keep it number one.

THE WARNING

You hypocrites! Well did Isaiah prophesy of you, when he said:
"This people honor me with their lips,
but their heart is far from me',

Matthew 15:7

7

Entice the Christian to walk in the flesh

If they walk in the spirit, they'll please God and influence men. So, set up every trap to entice them to walk in the flesh and the list are these:sexual immorality, impurity, and debauchery; idolatry and witchcraft; hatred, discord, jealousy, fits of rage, selfish ambition, dissensions, factions and envy; drunkenness and orgies. If Christians include these attributes in their lifestyle, they will condemn themselves, never yield any real fruit, become ineffective in their witness and their life will be laughable to the world and will never be able to stand against evil powers.

So, our job is to entice, them with the list.

Keep up the pressure to get them angry at their job, upset with their spouse, mad at their kids and frustrated with their ministry. If we can irritate them, we can affect them.

THE SOLUTION
But I say, walk by the Spirit,
and you will not carry out the desire of the flesh.

Galatians 5:16

8

Promote strife

Angry or bitter disagreement over fundamental issues; conflict.

Strife is the silent killer, you can't touch it, you can't see it, but you know when it is present, and you will always know who it's between and who is the cause of it. If we can get them to disagree with each other, we can come in.

Strife is usually birthed out of disagreement, so get them to disagree, sharply. People will always disagree but if we can cause them to take it to heart. We can cause strife; this can only be accomplished by placing a contentious person on staff. The aim of any contentious person is to get other people to agree with them. They will try to get people to side with them over any issue.

Strife is very important in the destruction of any church as it is the undercurrent that leads to separation.

Lot and Abraham had strife, and they had to separate.

So, strife will always lead to separation.

Where there is strife, there is confusion and every evil work. So, where there is disagreement in a church try to shift it to the next gear which is strife.

THE WARNING

For where envying and strife is, there is confusion and every evil work.

James 3:16

9

Use contentious people to sow discord

Contentious people are contagious. They are never happy until everyone else is unhappy. If they are placed anywhere in the ministry, they will either corrupt, disrupt or destroy that particular area. Contentious people are the key to infecting others with dissatisfaction.

Contentious people strive on disagreement.

Contentious people never want to see harmony.

Contentious people are unhappy people and will usually be the very people we work through to divide loyalty in a church.

Contentious people do not rest until they have stirred up people to rebel and their entry point is always conversation, so use them at any cost.

Contentious people can destroy any church, family, marriage, and workplace quickly. They are effective anywhere they are placed, and are far more effective if they are in a leadership role. So, look for the complainers, those that murmurer and backbite and use them.

Contentious people are usually at the forefront of church splits.

THE WARNING

Be not deceived: evil communications corrupt good manners.

1st Corinthians 15:33

10

Doctrinal differences

Create denominations that provoke more divisions. Cause them to argue over doctrinal differences and forget about the Gospel, the grace of God and the love of God. If Christians ever start loving the way God wants them to love we'll lose the war. Also, our tactics will become ineffective and useless if the church really starts loving one another the way God wants them to. So, let them promote their denomination more than they promote the cross, now it becomes more about what my church does than what Christ has done. So destroy their love walk by bringing about doctrinal differences.

Create so many denominations it becomes confusing to genuine seekers.

THE SOLUTION
Have nothing to do with foolish, ignorant controversies; you know that they breed quarrels.

2 Timothy 2:23

11

Give them a desire for the supernatural but no desire to learn the Bible

The supernatural is everywhere, television, books, movies, etc. The gospel is supernatural. Jesus birth, life, death, and resurrection are supernatural. Therefore, give them a strong desire for the supernatural, for the gifts and the power, but place little enthuses on sound biblical teaching.

So, if they are not careful, they'll cast out devils but spread doctrinal error, prophecy your name and address but know nothing about the Bible.

These people will often end up in error as they are hungry for the power of God but lack in the knowledge of scriptures. This is dangerous for the Christian because when they are going through tough times the power of God won't keep them only the knowledge and application of God's Word can do that, so keep them ignorant of the word of God.

THE WARNING

Many will say to me in that day, Lord, Lord, have we not prophesied in thy name? and in thy name have cast out devils? and in thy name done many wonderful works? And then will I profess unto them, I never knew you: depart from me, ye that work iniquity.

Matthew 7:22-23

12

Promote the novice quickly

When some experience a new life in Christ many are quick to want to change the world, so we let them, but to change the world, they'll believe they need a title.

So, we encourage leaders to promote new converts quickly, usually to a level that they are not ready for.

So now we have people who are saved for a year, and now they call themselves a pastor, converted for six months, and they are now an apostle, recently baptised and now they want to open their own church. They may have a great zeal, and some may even possess some spiritual gifts but if they have not received any real training, are not grounded in the things of God and have no real solid foundation, pride will set in quickly, and the fall is imminent. Many have become shipwreck by falling for this tactic. When novices are promoted, it will usually do more harm than good.

THE WARNING

An elder must not be a new believer, because he might become proud, and the devil would cause him to fall.

1st Timothy 3:6

13

Promote religion and legalism over personal relationship

Religion is the enemy of a relationship with God, and it is this very thing that can destroy a person walk with the Lord. Religion will allow people to come to church but never experience real change. So, people will come in spiritually dead and leave the same. Formalism is a killer to any church when they embrace formalism, they will never embrace anything new. There are many who are still living under the letter of the law and not enjoying the Christian life, they are bound by dos and don'ts and prize religion over relationship. When a religious spirit abounds in a church no one is changed, they go in the same and come out the same.

In this church

- Psychology and psychiatry replace discernment
- Eloquence replaces the demonstration of the power of God
- Administrators replace Prophets and Apostles
- Reason and logic replace living by faith
- Motivational preaching replaces the message of the Cross
- Entertainment replaces power

Their excuse for these changes will be because the church is moving into the 21st century and needs to embrace change.

But when they move in this direction, it is a change for the worse.

Promote religion at all cost.

THE SOLUTION

Do not be amazed that I said, 'You must be born again.' The wind blows where it wishes. You hear its sound, but you do not know where it comes from or where it is going. So it is with everyone born of the Spirit."

John 3:7-8

14

No Vision

Without a vision, the people perish.

There are church's with big visions to heal the sick, deliver those that are bound, build schools, feed the poor and other such things, but there are some churches who have not got a clue. They just have a desire to go to church but have no vision for the future. When there is nothing to work for, then the people have nothing to strive towards. Christianity now becomes mundane. They are just going to church, going to work, going to church, going to work a repetitive pattern of boredom.

When people have goals, they have something to get up for; they have something to live for, a zeal for life, and a desire to achieve and make a real difference.

When they forget God's goal and God's agenda which is the Great Commission, the church now becomes a social club for people that say they love Jesus but never do anything for Jesus.

First Century Christians lost their lives and were happy to do so, fast forward 2000 years later and their vision is now for a car, a house, prestige, fame and a desire to make it big.

That has now become the Christians vision for their life. If they ever get a godly vision, they must never complete it, delay, derail and destroy any vision that they may try to accomplish. If they begin to build on their vision, they must never agree on how to achieve it, sow the spirit of discord to destroy it.

THE SOLUTION

Where there is no vision, the people are unrestrained,
But happy is he who keeps the law.

Proverbs 29:18

15

Puff the gifted Ones
(An old favourite)

There are gifted people everywhere. People find they have a flare to sing, preach, play, and their gift will become noticed. So, you go to work on their ego through the power of suggestion, find the seed of pride and water it. When people keep telling them how good they are, it will start off with them shrugging it off, but as time goes on, if they don't keep their heart right, after a while they'll begin to think it's all about them. Sooner or later if they are not humble, they'll start to walk in pride. Then you'll have them to believe the church cannot run without them, if they can obtain a clique (following in the church) even better, those around them will value their opinion more than the pastors. If the pastor tries to correct the flamboyant one, any attack on their friend will seem like an attack on them.

Now they have popularity with people when they leave the church, and they'll take others with them. Because of their experience they'll believe ministry is easy and want to start their own church, resulting in ministries that God did not start and which God is not a part of.

THE WARNING

But when he had become powerful, he also became proud, which led to his downfall.

2nd Chronicles 26:16

If you cannot influence them to rebel, put to work plan B;

16

Offer the gifted Ones the world

Those endowed with a powerful gift, singing, music, prophetic, etc.; offer them any price necessary to abort their mission, so we can use their gift for our gain. If we can't destroy their gifting, then we must offer the necessary price so we can buy it.

If it is singing offer them a (secular)record contract so they'll sing about all kinds of profanity but go on to acknowledge God at an awards ceremony.

If it is a supernatural gift entice them to use it for money.

Christ saw through the temptations, however many of his follower's fail to recognise it when it comes. So, offer them, fame, money, women, men, record contracts, whatever their lust is work on it and use it to get what we want. But don't let them use their gift in the Kingdom, it will advance the gospel and weaken our influence.

THE WARNING

"I will give you the glory of these kingdoms and authority over them," the devil said, "because they are mine to give to anyone I please.

Luke 4:6

17

Promote a people friendly Gospel

Use a people-friendly gospel to keep people comfortable Promote the 'We are not here to hurt anybody Gospel.'

These churches are increasing in number; don't preach about sin, repentance, holiness, hell or eternal judgement.

This people friendly gospel dares not offend anyone or tread on anyone's toes. This gospel accepts everyone just the way they and encourages no one to change.

This gospel is a great weapon, so if they ever hear the real gospel that preaches the message of the Cross, the Grace of God, eternal life as well as the consequence of sin, judgement and hell they'll reject it and call the preacher old fashioned and condemning.

This gospel is more you can change (but without God) this friendly Gospel will allow people to stay comfortable in the sin they're in, in turn keeping them bound and blindfolded to the truth and whilst going to hell.

THE WARNING

They say to the seers, "Do not see," and to the prophets," Do not prophesy the truth to us. Tell us flattering things.
Prophesy illusions.

Isaiah 30:10

18

Promote a bless me Gospel

This gospel works best in the west and is spreading. There must be a strong enthuses that God is going to bless you message. Yes, there is truth in this, but if that is all they hear when they experience persecution, hard times and ridicule they'll give up, it's called the thorny ground mentality.

When persecution arises because of the word sake, they are 'offended' and fall away. If they think Christianity is just a good time, they won't endure hardships. They'll faint at chastisement, leave when rebuked and fall away when tempted. So, cause them to hear the message 'God is going to bless you.' When they don't get the blessing, they have been asking for at the time they expect to receive it, they'll become bitter and hard done by, forgetting they will receive all these blessings with persecution.

THE WARNING

The seed falling on rocky ground refers to someone who hears the word and at once receives it with joy. But since they have no root, they last only a short time. When trouble or persecution comes because of the word, they quickly fall away.

Matthew 13:20-21

19

The promotion of homosexuality and persecution of the Church

Times are changing. These days we use all forms of media to promote the homosexual lifestyle, and as it continues to grow, weak churches will feel intimidated to preach against sin, and instead look for a way of inclusion, for fear of persecution and how they will be treated if they speak out against this sin. They will rather keep quiet and dance around the issue. While the world system promotes it, When the church stays silent about the problem, the sin grows, leaders become increasingly intimidated by it, the spread of homosexuality will permeate society and by the time they do realise its far-reaching effects it would of already have been a force to reckon with, thus making this sin the guiding factor in the fight against Christianity.

So raise up powerful homosexuals in places of influence in government, media, education, health, science, sports and most importantly music, which will cause people to accept the lifestyle because their idols promote it.

Now because everyone else accepts it, it will make it hard for the church to preach against it and when they do, persecution will await them, their church, their family and their business. This attack is a strategic one which will take all the forces working together to bring about the end goal, the destruction of Christianity.

The fear of persecution will cause established churches to sidestep big social issues facing society.

IF THEY ARE A STRONG CHURCH, THEY WILL PREACH THE TRUTH IF THEY ARE A WEAK CHURCH THEY WILL COMPROMISE

THIS WILL DETERMINE WHO IS REALLY PREACHING BIBLICAL CHRISTIANITY

THE WARNING

Do you not know that the unrighteous will not inherit the kingdom of God? Do not be deceived. Neither fornicators, nor idolaters, nor adulterers, nor homosexuals nor sodomites, nor thieves, nor covetous, nor drunkards, nor revilers, nor extortioners will inherit the kingdom of God.

1 Corinthians 6:9-10

20

Influence the Christian to work outside the timing of God

It is easy to tempt a person with something God has already promised them. If God has promised the Christian something, God will usually work in his own time to bring it to pass, because God has promised them something. Our job is to get them to make it happen before the appointed time. When this happens, they run ahead of God and work outside his timing and end up somewhere they should be not at a time they should not be there with an anointing they do not yet carry. It has been done many times. For this, to work, we use people to encourage them that this is their time. So, we use the 'Power of Suggestion.' Abraham being an excellent example, Sarah tried to make it happen for Abraham by offering him, Hagar. The effects are still being felt in the Middle East today. So, we use well-meaning people to influence the Christian to run ahead of God and try to make it happen themselves.

There are people called to lead, but they have never submitted to anyone, there are people called to be Prophets and pastors but are not aware that God has a process. So, they go out before their time. These people are oblivious to the fact that if they promote themselves, they will have to maintain themselves.

Influence the Christian to work outside the timing of God.

THE SOLUTION
Wait on the LORD: be of good courage, and he shall strengthen thine heart: wait, I say, on the LORD.

Psalms27:14

21

Promote competition amongst ministers

This point is also promoted through people.

You hear it all the time that minister has a bigger church, a bigger car, a nicer house, an international ministry; this minister is being invited to address the government, and influencing kings.

When one minister is being used in areas of prominence and receiving international significance, some people instead of celebrating that man or woman, if their heart is not right it will usually ignite the green-eyed devil of envy which births jealousy. So now the competition starts.

That minister has a 5-bedroom house; I must have a 10-bedroom house.

That church has 5000 members; I must have 10,000.

That minister has a Mercedes; I must have a Bentley.

That minister is on television; I must own my own channel.

This is the old age problem among human beings "who wants to be greatest" this also causes ministers to lose their focus of what God has called them to do, and they begin to contemplate what others are achieving.

It now becomes about personal ambition and not the will of God. This can only be accomplished if they are focused on what others are doing and not listening to what God is saying. We must keep their focus on others, so we continue to bombard them with stories of what other people are doing and what other ministries are achieving. Instead of focusing on God's assignment for their lives they'll play keeping up with the Jones.

If you cannot destroy a ministry then distracts them from their purpose. Mission Accomplished.

THE WARNING

We do not dare to classify or compare ourselves with some who commend themselves. When they measure themselves by themselves and compare themselves with themselves,
they are not wise.

2 Corinthians 10:12

22

Glamorize a particular ministry over another

For this to work, make the minister believe what he or she is called to do is not effective. Let them become bored with what they have been called to do. Now the Pastor wants to be Evangelist, the Teacher wants to be a Prophet, the businessman wants to be Pastor, and the banker wants to be an Apostle. Eventually, if they're not careful they'll be drawn to do something God did not call them to do; Result they will be ineffective and waste their years outside of the will of God.

This can only succeed by making a particular ministry look more exciting than what they are doing. Poorly paid pastors have left the call of God because of six-figure job. Evangelists have become pastors as they become fed up travelling. Business people have left their business to start a ministry, not knowing that God had called them to the market place and that is where they will be most effective. Most of the time the key element here is the lure is money, yes, they may have more money but will never be completely satisfied or be truly effective or fulfil the will of God for their lives.

THE SOLUTION
And the world passes away, and the lust thereof: but he that does the will of God abides forever.

1st John 2:17

23

Use ministers to attack other Ministers

Get ministers to share deep secrets about one another and their congregation, these secrets are shared under the guise of prayer, but really, it's called spiritualized gossip. When the secrets are shared then it's your job to cause division and disagreement between the ministers, this must be made so contentious that what they shared together as friends which was at one time deep guarded secret can quickly become public knowledge, to the detriment of each other's ministries, what's more when people hear the gossip people will believe the news as it would have come from a trusted source. For this, to work, we must go to work on the relationship in the church, and amongst themselves, so we use strife, contention, misunderstanding, and miscommunication, use everything to divide and conquer the rest will follow. If successful these particular methods are ongoing and can be repeated at random.

When non-Christians see Christians tearing each other apart, they themselves will want no part in Christianity. This becomes a tool to keep sinners away from the Kingdom of God.

THE WARNING

For you are yet carnal: for while there is among you envying, and strife, and divisions, are you not carnal, and walk as men?

1st Corinthians 3:3

24

Frustration

Do your best to frustrate the pastor with everything you can. Remind the pastor that the church is not growing, the people are not growing, the people are not giving, people are not dedicated, wife (or husband) does not understand, the children are not listening; the people aren't responding, etc. Do everything in your power to frustrate him/her. The frustration can sometimes lead to a sense of hopelessness and desperation, which will birth the thoughts of giving up and some will even begin to harness doubts if God really called them.

THE COUNTER ATTACK
Be anxious for nothing, but in everything by prayer and supplication with thanksgiving let your requests be made known to God.

Philippians 4:6

25

Place the wrong person over the finances

Remember Judas, had the money bag. So, let them chose friendship over financial management. Churches are unaware that the person in charge of the financial department must be blameless, integral and sober, anything less than that will result in a problem. If the person in this department is not kept in check, it will soon unravel.

So, give the person over the finances a financial problem that means their problem must be: They have no money.

When this is in place, we introduce the temptation. As temptation sets in, those without money and the absence of the fear of the Lord it is now an accident waiting to happen.

THE WARNING
But Israel violated the instructions about the things set apart for the LORD. A man named Achan had stolen some of these dedicated things, so the LORD was very angry with the Israelites.
Achan was the son of Carmi, a descendant of Zimri son of Zerah, of the tribe of Judah.

Joshua 7:1

26

Use strong financial members to control the leader

This particular scheme works best if the pastor is broke. If he is easily influenced and doesn't like offending people even better.

If the leader notices that he has strong financial givers who seem to be sustaining the ministry, get him to tread carefully. Not to preach to offend them, if they get offended, they might leave the church and leave a gap in the church finances.

When these financial backers begin to notice their influence, they will start to feel they have a say in the affairs of the church and begin to air them. A weak pastor will feel obligated to do what they want him to do and not what God is telling him to do. This particular scheme works even better when the finical backers are living in sin and a lifestyle contrary to the word of God. The pastor will tiptoe around their sin, preferring instead to keep them in his church than rebuking them for their wrongdoing.

THIS WORKS BEST WHEN THE PASTOR HAS FORGOTTEN THAT GOD IS HIS SOURCE NOT MAN.

THE WARNING
You rulers make decisions based on bribes; you priests teach God's laws only for a price; you prophets won't prophesy unless you are paid. Yet all of you claim to depend on the LORD...

Micah 3:11

27

Character assassination

If you can assassinate the character of the leader or the people around him/her, this will cause discouragement and possibly cause them to harbor thoughts of giving up and leave the ministry. When assassinating someone's character it is always good to use people close to them, the reason is twofold, it makes what they say more believable and discourages the victim even more so, this will cause the leader to not trust anyone and will be dubious of everyone around them, they will never able to share their heart with anyone again.

Note: Character assassination works better on younger ministers as they are more concerned with what people believe about them, older ministers are wiser and recognize its attack, so work on the younger minister, this will usually bring discouragement.

Character assassination is simple; promote lies about the person you are trying to destroy.

The internet is a valuable resource in assassinating the character of a minister. People will believe anything they have seen on YouTube and read on Facebook.

THE COUNTER ATTACK

A good name is to be chosen rather than great riches, and favor is better than silver or gold

Proverbs 22:1

28

Cause them to blame God for the bad things that happen

You have heard it over and over again. If there was a God, why did he let this happen to me? It's has been working for years, now intensify the assault on the mind.

Earthquakes, floods, wars, disasters, famines, pestilence, plagues, to mention a few, build up the picture that if God is such a good God why are so many bad things happening? Disguise who the author of all evil is and cause them to blame God for everything wrong that happens in their life.

This can only happen if people are not acquainted with the character and love of God and do not know the scriptures.

So, when everything bad happens, plant thoughts in their mind "this is Gods fault". Job saw through this and was not ignorant to this particular trap, many, however, are not.

So, when their marriage breaks down, blame God.

When their child becomes sick, they blame God.

When they lose their Job, blame God.

When they lose their house, blame God.

When everything goes wrong, infect their mind to think the worse.

This has been working for years. When people fall for this they have forgotten the scriptures and believe the lie.

THE COUNTER ATTACK:

The thief does not come except to steal, and to kill, and to destroy. I have come that they may have life, and that they may have it more abundantly.

John 10:10

29

Reminders of the past

To really infiltrate the believer, we must continue to bring the sins of their past back to them every now and again, (we go for a season) continue to observe their life and then at their lowest point bring them the temptations of the past. Drugs, lust, pornography whatever held them before we can get them again if they're not on fire. When they fall, then we use our special...Condemnation.

What they fail to realize is the same voice that tempted them to sin is the same voice that turns around and condemns them when they sin.

Temptation works best when they give way to discouragement. Discouragement is the launch pad to weariness, which will give way to fainting in their minds.

THE SOLUTION

Brethren, I count not myself to have apprehended: but this one thing I do, forgetting those things which are behind, and reaching forth unto those things which are before,

Philippians 3:13

30

Discourage the workers

Make the workers feel undervalued. Humans are so gullible; they always need a well done or some recognition. When they feel undervalued eventually, they'll forget that they are doing this for God and become weary in well doing. The result will be that they'll stop doing it altogether or do it with half a heart.

Incline the workers to believe they are doing this for the church or the pastor if they are ever rebuked or corrected or spoken to in a way they don't like they'll become offended and drop the job. As laborers are needed in the church, cause them to hire volunteers who have not been vetted in character and people who are not really converted, before you know it we'll have people working in the church who are surface Christians living double lives, which leaves a door open to wreak havoc in other areas.

THE COUNTER ATTACK
They were just trying to intimidate us, imagining that they could discourage us and stop the work. So I continued the work with even greater determination.

Nehemiah 6:9

31

Distraction

If you can't destroy them, distract them. They must not fulfil God's will for their life. So send people in to deter the leader's focus.

The best schemes which cause the greatest distractions are the Get-Rich-Schemes, You can make money doing this, and this idea can make you rich.

These schemes are a dime a dozen, the person leading the distraction should always come under the guise of 'this scheme will help your church.'

It will start off subtle then the scheme will take up all the pastors' time, even better if it brings in money, we could take him/her away from his ministry altogether if they not grounded in the faith. Use men to distract the women, and the women to distract the men, use money to distract the covetous, use rumours to distract the weak, whatever you do remember distraction is the key to an unfulfilled goal if you can't destroy, distract.

THE SOLUTION

Looking unto Jesus the author and perfecter of our faith; who for the joy that was set before him endured the cross, despising the shame, and is seated at the right hand of the throne of God.

Hebrews 12:2

32

Disgruntled ex-members

The crème de la crème in discrediting a church.
The disgruntled, offended unhappy ex-member. People leave church all the time; some reasons are stronger than others. Which promote stronger feelings; many are being driven out with unforgiveness, bitterness, anger and hatred.

When an ex-member is unhappy with their once beloved church most of the time, we don't have to do much, they'll do it all themselves. They will gossip, slander and expose wrongdoings. Such stories are considered concrete evidence if coming from the mouth of those who were once close to the ministry.

Bitterness is a launch pad for Tell-All-Stories when people are bitter, they will reveal stories that were once held a secret. Bitterness is the root of a fruit called revenge. Bitter people get even. So, they will contact newspapers, television people and spew out every last ounce of negativity about your organisation.

Disgruntled Ex-Members are a valuable tool in our hands,
USE THEM AT ALL COST.

THE WARNING
Even my close friend whom I trusted, he who shared meals with me, has turned against me.

Psalm 41:9

33

Miserable door staff

It seems simple and almost too easy, but its effects are far-reaching.

Place someone unwelcoming at the door of the church. Make sure they are cold, uncaring and uninviting. Simple tactics such as these are self-destructive issues the church is doing to bury their own ministry.

First impressions last, most people will never come back if you place the wrong face at the door. In fact, for maximum effect, make the whole church unwelcoming, so when people step into the church no one shakes your hand, no one smiles at you, no asks how you are, first-time visitors are not welcomed. When people act like this, they are ensuring that first-time visitors actually become one- and only-time visitors.

When Christians are miserable and uncaring, no one enjoying their sinful lifestyle will want to give it up and join an unhappy bunch of people.

Miserable door staff and unhappy Christians are the self-destruct button for any church.

THE SOLUTION
Rejoice in the Lord always: and again I say, Rejoice.

Philippians 4:4

34

Baggage from their last ministry

People leave church all the time; few leave the right way, most leave the wrong way, offended, hurt, upset, angry and unresolved issues with their last pastor. Anyone with common sense knows that nothing is settled unless it is settled right, but pride, un-forgiveness, and indifference make this impossible. So most of the time they fail to realize that the problem has not been left behind, but is actually inside them. It's called offence.

If left unchecked the root of bitterness will defile them, and now they are another pastor's problem.

THE WARNING

Keep thy heart with all diligence; for out of it are the issues of life.

Proverbs 4:23

35

Promote the anointing and wisdom imbalance in the church

Create an anointing/wisdom imbalance in the church.

Let me explain, there are men anointed to heal the sick, but have no idea about finances. There are ministers casting out devils and delivering the afflicted but still renting a hall after 10 years. They can discern the spiritual world keenly but can't pay their bills. Can prophesy accurately, but cannot find the finances for a mortgage. Why because the sought out the anointing and forgot about wisdom, they promoted the power of God but failed on gaining knowledge. Likewise, there are churches with great structure and perfect order, but no anointing. There are prestigious choirs and beautiful buildings, but the presence of God is not there. We have infiltrated these churches easily because there is no anointing and if there is no anointing, there is no power. This imbalance is found frequently all over the world, if we can keep them ignorant to this imbalance, we'll have anointed men and woman who can preach up a storm but make little impact only affecting their community and not the world and boring preachers with mass choirs, large congregations with people who go in church one way and come out the same. No change.

Keep them ignorant

THE SOLUTION

Wisdom is the principal thing, therefore get wisdom: and with all thy getting get understanding.

Proverbs 4:7

How God anointed Jesus of Nazareth with the Holy Spirit and with power, who went about doing good and healing all that were oppressed of the devil, for God was with him.

Acts 10:38

36

Cause the church to major on the minors

Cause the church to argue over petty things, and make these petty things big things, dress code, hairstyles, tattoos, where they go and where they can't go and cause them to leave off the important things like fasting and prayer, soul winning and seeking the face of God, the baptism of the Holy Ghost.

Cause them to have a debate about everything and meetings about nothing.

When they major on the minors and blew up the little things, it discourages people who are serious about seeking God. When they major on the minors, everything becomes a problem, and everything is an issue.

THE WARNING

"What sorrow awaits you Pharisees! For you are careful to tithe even the tiniest income from your herb gardens, but you ignore justice and the love of God. You should tithe, yes, but do not neglect the more important things.

Luke 11:42

37

Make the church lookout of touch

Promote the image that the church and its message are no longer relevant, either by making them look so dated no one will want to join or cause them to be so carnal, they become a mirror image of the world, either which way, they must look out of touch and dated, and their message must not be relevant today.

So, make the message boring and long. No power no presence.

Now when people come to church, sadly, all the visitors look forward to is the tea and biscuits at the end.

THE SOLUTION
Jesus Christ is the same yesterday, today, and forever.

Hebrews 13:8

38

Isolate the leader

Isolation is the pathway to elimination when a leader has no one to turn to, speak to, confide in or learn from that leader is on the path to nowhere. The leader that has no one to speak and turn to will usually make foolish decisions, without counsel they will lean on their own understanding and make rash decisions without much thought to the outcome, The key to isolation is that it makes it impossible to receive care from others, leaders who are significantly isolated limit their learning and a leader that is not learning is not growing, this will greatly limit their effectiveness and leave them making little impact and lastly isolated leaders will usually become divorced from reality, so they lead in ways that are out of sync with reality. Any predatory animal will know that it is effortless to attack a lone prey. So, before the attack, isolation must be in place. Now they are left to battle with their thoughts, and when things really heat up, they can begin to question themselves. Did God really call me? Did I really hear from heaven? Is this really what God wants from me?

THE SOLUTION
The God of Israel dictated unto me, the strong One of Israel spoke):
He that rules over men must be just, ruling in the fear of God.

2 Samuel 23:3

39

Promote false conversions

They love the church, the pastor, the people; they love the services, the singing, and their friends attend the church. So, these become the foundation on which the Christian convert has built their faith upon. However, when the going gets tough, the trials will reveal their heart.

When they lose their job will they still come to church, when their friends leave church they will follow them out the door? When a message comes that deals with their sin will they become offended and leave? If they fall sick and no one from their church goes to see them will they become bitter and angry at God and the church? If they have no relationship with God, they'll leave church bitter and angry.

THE WARNING

The seeds on the rocky soil represent those who hear the message and receive it with joy. But since they don't have deep roots, they believe for a while, thenthey fall away when they face temptation.

Luke 8:13

40

Pride

Pride is the number one weapon against anyone wanting to accomplish great things for God. Pride has caused many a great man and woman to fall, pride has destroyed many ministries and ruined many lives. Pride blinds the heart and causes people to lean on their own might and ability. When pride sets in men forget who to give the glory to. If they're oblivious to this pride will creep in and set up residence in the heart. The weapon of Pride rarely fails; the problem with pride is the person who has it is usually the last to know, but always the first to see it in others.

God is using me, I am God's man, and it's all about me.

The danger of Pride is that it is the only sin that can come in when people are doing the will of God. You can actually be doing what you are supposed to be doing but then forget whose power is enabling you to do what you are doing.

Pride is dangerous as it listens to no one.

A proud person believes they are always right.

A proud person will never take correction.

A proud person will always try to turn around a situation to make themselves appear better than everyone else.

A proud person never ever apologizes or admits wrong doing.

Remember pride feeds off compliments and accolades, so bombard them with how great they are, how humble they are, and how anointed they are, etc. Sooner or later if not careful and they don't give God the glory, Pride will take a seat, and a fall is imminent.

THE WARNING

But when he had become powerful, he also became proud, which led to his downfall. He sinned against the LORD his God by entering the sanctuary of the LORD's Temple and personally burning incense on the incense altar.

2 Chronicles 26:16

41

Never cause the backslider to return

If the backslider can stay out long enough, we can destroy them, remember God has not finished with the backslider, he still wants them back. There are seven devils are waiting for every Christian who decides to go back, those seven devils are the key to destroying the backslider and ensuring they never return. Many do return, however, if we can destroy them before returning to God, mission accomplished. So, use every conceivable bait necessary in keeping them out of the Kingdom of God. Use the boyfriend, girlfriend, shame, condemnation, pride, un-forgiveness and money, whatever it may be. Just keep them content singing the same song 'I'm not ready yet.' When they keep confessing that they will never be ready and when they least expect it, we'll snatch them and watch them fall into eternity without Christ.

THE COUNTER ATTACK

The Lord is not slack concerning his promise, as some men count slackness; but is longsuffering to us-ward, not willing that any should perish, but that all should come to repentance.

2nd Peter 3:9

42

Jezebel: The master manipulator

Let the church keep believing that Jezebel is female in a short skirt or skimpy dress waiting to seduce who she can, so they stay vigilant for the seductress female but miss the associate minister whose secret ambition is to topple leadership and assume his/her position. Many churches have Jezebel confused. Many churches miss the controlling minister or the one that becomes disruptive and vindictive when they don't get their own way. Use the person's character flaws and sin to enter in. A person with a Jezebel spirit will never admit wrong unless it is a temporary admittance of guilt to gain "favor" with someone. Jezebel takes credit for everything. The Spirit of Jezebel lets others do its dirty work. The Jezebel spirit is a form of witchcraft and witchcraft spirits loves to control people and will do anything to retain power; Jezebel will remove others to gain its control. A classic ploy of a controller is to ignore you when you disagree with him. This tactic is frequently used by leaders when someone doesn't agree with their plans, they then isolate the person by ignoring them. Since a Jezebel is never wrong if you disagree with her get ready to become her worst enemy. As long as you are in agreement with her, all is fine, but if you challenge her, then look out. You are now the number one target for its destruction.

This spirit criticizes everyone. A Jezebel is a master at belittling another person to make themselves look good. A person with a Jezebel spirit is threatened by the prophetic. The reason being is that someone with a prophetic gift or ministry will be able to identify the Jezebel Spirit and will cast it out. Remember Jezebel in the Bible tried to destroy all the true prophets of God. So, let Jezebel wreak havoc silently by using the person eager for leadership.

Jezebel is a control freak, if she is given any leadership role, it is the beginning of the end for that church.

If she is tolerated, she'll destroy.
Jezebels greatest enemy is a Jehu.

THE WARNING

Nevertheless I have a few things against you, because you allow that woman Jezebel, who calls herself a prophetess, to teach and to seduce my servants to commit fornication, and to eat things sacrificed unto idols.

Revelation 2:20

43

Absalom: The heart stealer

Absalom was the son of David sat near the gate of the city and looked for people who were discontented or had problems, He would sympathize with them and would eventually get the people (including the top people) to side with him, and this took place until he overthrew his father. This spirit is magnificent at getting people to side with them and excellent at gaining peoples affection. Absalom always has a contrary vision to the one of the house, excellent at gathering others for support and master at stealing the hearts of the people. Division is King in the heart of those with the Absalom spirit, we can use Absalom because an Absalom Spirit is rooted in a basic distrust and resentment of God-ordained authority. An Absalom Spirit is rooted in hidden agendas, hidden strategies and hidden hatred for leadership camouflaged with a strong desire to take their place. An Absalom Spirit manifests itself in self-promotion and self-advancement, use Absalom at all cost. The use of this spirit is again twofold, we use the rebel to overtake and overthrow, and we use pain offense to hurt the one being overthrown. It works every time.

THE WARNING

Then Absalom would say, "You've really got a strong case here! It's too bad the king doesn't have anyone to hear it. I wish I were the judge. Then everyone could bring their cases to me for judgment, and I would give them justice!"

2 Samuel 15:3-4

44

They must never be allowed to recognize their authority as believers

Their saviour died and rose again he has given them the victory, dominion, power, and authority; however, many are oblivious to this fact. We must keep them blinded to the truth of the authority they really hold. If they ever get a hold of the fact, they have dominion over us through that name our plans are thwarted, and our kingdom will come under attack. So, keep them ignorant, don't let them read, listen, watch, pray or do anything that will cause them to reveal the power they have.

Give them a desire for a good time in church (jumping, shouting, hooping, etc.) but never come away with real teaching which is able to impact their lives. They must never recognize the authority they hold. If the Christian uses their authority, we'll lose ground and our dominion in the earth.

THE SOLUTION

Behold, I give unto you power to tread on serpents and scorpions, and over all the power of the enemy: and nothing shall by any means hurt you.

Luke 10:19

45

Fight against the ministries which demonstrate healing and deliverance

These ministries must be stopped at all cost. Our job is to inflict as much pain and suffering on mankind as possible. If these ministries that demonstrate healing and deliverance continue to grow our work will be destroyed. These ministries are our number one enemy in the world. So, we throw everything at these churches. Slander, Gossip, betrayal, bring media attention to their crazy practices, persecute them from all sides, from within and from without. Whip up scandalous stories which will deter people from attending these churches. The fight against healing and deliverance must be relentless. If these preachers keep casting demons out, they stop our work in the earth. So dumb down every sickness, mental health is physiological, not spiritual. Depression is clinical, not the spirit of heaviness. That sickness is a fact of life people must accept, and not something that can be treated supernaturally. This bombardment of the church will cause people to lose faith in God's word and cause people with real problems to try their luck in other help (witch doctors, white magic, etc.) Which are our agents on the earth.

So do whatever it takes to stop these churches operating in the supernatural power of God.

Healing and deliverance is our greatest enemy uses every trick in the book to see it shut down.

THE SOLUTION

And I say also unto thee, That thou art Peter, and upon this rock I will build my church; and the gates of hell shall not prevail against it.

Matthew 16:18

46

They must never be allowed to recognize the power of praise and worship

If they ever realize the power of Praise and worship, we won't be able to get near them. God inhabits the praise of his people. He literally lives in their praises. Praise gets their focus off themselves, and back on God, as praise usually brings joy if they praise him, they'll begin to get happy about everything and anything. When people praiseGod, there is no room for murmuring and complaining. Praise causes the enemy to flee and opens the door to Gods presence, and his presence is the gateway to his goodness. When people begin to praise God, they open up the heavens and miracles start to happen, prison doors open, and people get set free. There are countless scenarios in the bible were Gods people experienced the supernatural by praising and worshiping God. So keep them bound by causing them never to open their mouth.

THE COUNTER ATTACK
And when they began to sing and to praise, the LORD set ambushes against the children of Ammon, Moab, and mount Seir, who were come against Judah; and they were defeated.

2 Chronicles 20:22

47

If they get saved, they must never renew their mind

Let them go to church, sing songs, but they must never start thinking in line with God's word. To change a man's life, you must first change his mind. There are millions of people that go to church every week, but their lives are not changed. If these people meditate on the word and begin to implement what they hear we will have a real problem on our hands. So, let them ever be hearing but never coming to the knowledge of the truth. If they go to seminars, they must never implement what they hear. If they listen to CD's and podcast, they must never come away with any real revelation.

They must not renew their mind; Mind renewal must be hindered and if possible, stopped at all cost.

A renewed mind gives way to a new man.

THE SOLUTION

And do not be conformed to this world, but be transformed by the renewing of your mind, so that you may prove what the will of God is, that which is good and acceptable and perfect.

Romans 12:2

48

Promote replacement theory

They must not understand the significance of the role the Jews play in their faith and the heritage they have. Abraham was a Jew, so to was Isaac, Jacob, Moses, Joshua, Samuel, David, Jeremiah, Isaiah, Samson, Peter, Paul and of course the Lord Jesus Christ, the bible is a book written by Jews, salvation is of the Jews, but many have forgotten the role of the Jews in scripture, So promote the idea that the Christian church has replaced the Jews. Many have fallen for this false teaching. They must never know the blessing that comes with blessing the Jews. They must never know if they bless the Jewish people they will be blessed. We must continue to fuel the media with pro-Palestinian media, and the terrible atrocities being committed in Israel. Continue to make the news one-sided against Israel. The world has fallen for it, so too will the churches if they are not careful. So, allow the church believe they have replaced the Jews, leaving them deluded. It's quite clear by scriptures that God has not forgotten the Jews, but if people believe the media more than they do God's word, they will fall for the lie.

THE SOLUTION

I ask, then, has God rejected his own people, the nation of Israel? Of course not! I myself am an Israelite, a descendant of Abraham and a member of the tribe of Benjamin.

Romans 11:1

49

Promote racism

Racism is on the rise all over the world. We know that slavery was used for four hundred years; the Europeans took Africans to the North and South America and the Caribbean and used them to build their wealth. Along with slavery, they introduced Christianity; although slavery is over, the effects of slavery linger on. Slavery is still a fundamental reason why some people of color reject Christianity. So, keep promoting the idea Christianity is a white man's religion to enslave people.

Hide the fact that Muslims also enslaved many Africans. Let them promote the transatlantic slave trade, but dumb down the Islamic slave trade across the Sahara, the Red Sea, and the Indian Ocean.

Embed it in the minds that the transatlantic slave trade lasted 400 years, but hide the facts that the Arab involvement in the slave trade lasted fourteen centuries.

This way it continues to be a black and white issue.

Racism is the great weapon on the rise in the world, if we can fuel the fire of racism we can continue to divide and conquer. So, we keep them divided by using the past. Let them argue over the outward appearance of Christ and forget that salvation comes through his blood.

THE SOLUTION

There is neither Jew nor Greek, there is neither slave nor free man, there is neither male nor female; for you are all one in Christ Jesus

Galatians 3:28

50

Use the abuse committed by some ministers to discredit their belief

The abuse by some priest is being widely publicized, with men like these in the church there is little more we need to do, these men are doing our work for us.

Their acts have destroyed the lives of many; they themselves are on their way to hell, so with behavior like this no one wins.

When the stories are publicized the majority loses faith in the church, and its message and people are hardened to the news of the gospel. Fewer and fewer people refuse to believe in the word the gospel offers due to the lousy representation of some of its ministers.

THE WARNING

"Woe to you, scribes and Pharisees, hypocrites! For you are like whitewashed tombs, which outwardly appear beautiful, but within are full of dead people's bones and all uncleanness. So you also outwardly appear righteous to others, but within you are full of hypocrisy and lawlessness.

Matthew 23:27-28

51

Attack the Mind

The mind is the human battleground and demons playground if they allow us in. This is where we plant thoughts, suggestions, ideas, and propositions, in the mind of the believer. It can all start with one thought. The entry into the mind is to start with the person's fears and insecurities.

Fear, we amplify problems in the mind by the power of suggestion, what they hear will affect their heart so we fill their ears with doubt, which will fill their heart with worry and anxiety, this then leads to fear and depression, Depression (aka the spirit of heaviness) begins to cloud the mind of the believer, causing them only to see hopelessness leading to despair, despair sees no way out, of the situation. Despair in the life of any human can become so overwhelming it can open the door to total destruction. There is always a pattern; it always begins gradually and subtlety. During this process, we would have been dropping subtle suggestions along the way. "It's useless, Why am I bothering? Just end it all, No one cares." These suggestions grow stronger and stronger, now the aim is to make these thoughts so loud in their mind it drowns out every other voice.

They have now become so convinced, not only do they think of giving up, they begin to say it, as death and life are in the words they speak, they have now begun to condemn themselves.

They have thought it, spoken it, now all that's left is for them to do it.

To drive them out of church.

Suggest that people don't like them, they're not appreciated, no one cares, and these thoughts will begin to taint their view. They will begin to see things that aren't really there. Soon they'll be saying "They're talking about me," "They don't like me," "I said hello, and they did not reply." These suggestions are the starting point for the big delusion they are about to walk into. As times goes on, we have played with their mind to such an extent that all they see is the negative. They will eventually begin to believe the lies and exit church.

THE SOLUTION

And be renewed in the spirit of your mind,

Ephesians 4:23

so that no advantage would be taken of us by Satan,
for we are not ignorant of his schemes.

2nd Corinthians 2:11

52

Make ministry look easy

Make ministry appear easy, that way those with a desire for ministry but have not been called to ministry will jump on the bandwagon, thinking anybody can do it. So, you'll have people who think they can have church without consulting God, producing ministries that are ineffective and man-made. This way, ministries are raised up that God didn't ordain, who poses the wrong motive and are in it for business and not the eternal destination of mankind. As these people will usually be immature, who sometimes may have a gift but very little on the way of character these are the very ministries that are leading people to a path called nowhere.

THE COUNTER ATTACK
And no one can become a high priest simply because he wants such an honor. He must be called by God for this work, just as Aaron was.

Hebrews 5:4

53

Make sex non-existent in the marriage of ministers

Keep the minister busy, Men and women. When people are busy, they begin to forget their duties, to their children and their spouse, when sex starts to become nonexistent in marriage the cracks will start to appear in the relationship. Sex is given by God and honored by God and is an essential part of marriage, so we keep them busy, let it always be about the ministry and work, work, work. Sooner or later one of them will feel neglected, and if they don't talk about it, it will soon become an issue. If they discuss the issue and one of the parties is still not willing to co-operate, now we have an avenue of which to walk through and cause havoc. Make the wife always tired and let the man never be home, if they don't have a relationship with God and they don't communicate with each other. We have a recipe for disaster. The inevitable will soon take place; Separation, possible adultery, divorce. So, use every conceivable trick to keep them from intimacy, let the phone always ring with someone wanting something, let them go on long trips frequently, keep meetings about everything and make sure they are always there. If they are both working and in ministry let them get so busy with their own lives, work and ministry the bedroom becomes a lonely place.

THE SOLUTION

But because of the temptation to sexual immorality, each man should have his own wife and each woman her own husband.

1st Corinthians 7:2

54

The Spear of Saul

The spear of Saul, as it has been coined, is an excellent weapon in destroying Christian fellowships; this tactic has, at its root the spirit of jealousy. The spear of Saul starts with suspicion; this is the leader that is suspicious of everyone and trusts no one. Insecurity is king in the heart of the person who possesses it.

This is a self-destructive trait which we can use to isolate and kill future leaders (and those around them aspiring for greatness). This type of leader wants people around but never wants to see them excel above themselves if they do this leader will secretly be planning their demise in order to make themselves appear better. The ulterior motive is at the heart of this leader, and they are never clear on anything or straight with anyone.

The object of the person wielding the spear is to assassinate any gift others may have that they themselves do not possess. The spear of Saul will try to set up others to fail, but the most enormous success this weapon causes is the rejection felt by those who are its target. The ultimate goal of this tactic is to discourage others and provoke them to run. Use the Spear of Saul at all cost, especially in Mentor/mentee relationships.

Saul was a leader who found himself on the wrong side of God when he disobeyed God; God rose up David to take his place, but in the interim Saul tried to kill David on more than one occasion. The Spear of Saul has a sharp edge called jealousy.

THE WARNING

And Saul sought to pin David to the wall with the spear, but he eluded Saul, so that he struck the spear into the wall. And David fled and escaped that night.

1st Samuel 19:10

55

Use the weapon of offence to keep them divided

Offence is killing the church, they sing, preach, evangelize, fast and pray, but in the hearts of many Christians, there is a root of offence eating them away.

Offence is causing division, strife, separation, church splits all over the world, and because nobody stops to examine their heart, everybody thinks they are in the right. The Spirit of offense springs into action when people have been hurt, insulted, mistreated, disrespected and overlooked, and when offense sets in, a wounded spirit is not far behind.

Offended people will usually do two things,

Stay in the church and infect other members with their poison or leave the church (with their offence) and find another church, without healing and confronting the hurt they feel, they will carry it to the next church and give that man of God their problem.

Seldom do people make amends with the person who has offended them. Many of them think they have gotten over it and they are healed, but the real test comes when they set their eyes on the person who has offended them, then they'll know if they are over it.

Offence is our greatest bait, let's use it at all cost. Let them have church just as long they're not united.

THE WARNING
A brother offended is more difficult than a fortified city; and disputes are like the bars of a fortress.

Proverbs 18:19

56

UNFORGIVENESS:
Hell's greatest weapon

Un-forgiveness is bringing more people to hell than the bullet. It is still the greatest Heaven blocker for many people. Many people do not know it or just too stubborn to forgive, either way, they keep this up they will never see heaven. It's written in the word. So, we get humans to amass as much hurt, pain, backbiting, slander, violence and evil as they can to each other, in the hope that they will never forgive each other for the pain they feel. Unforgiveness has a few negative traits attached to it namely sickness: If they harbor un-forgiveness long enough it will affect their body. It has been medically proven. So, we get them sick by getting them to hate each other.

Un-forgiveness prevents God from forgiving their sins if they do not forgive others God won't forgive them, so keep them bitter and remind them of what the other person did to them. Speak into their ears the pain they cause, works best for divorced people (some will never forgive,) people who have suffered injustice, hard done by, use any situation necessary to harbour resentment. Why because unforgiveness opens us up to the tormentors, when un-forgiveness is in their heart, we get free reign to come in and make their life hell, as un-forgiveness is a personal invitation for demons to enter. It will block God from answering their prayers, so they become the product of their own demise.

Un-forgiveness will keep a person out of heaven

THE WARNING

But if you do not forgive, neither will your Father which is in heaven forgive your trespasses.

Mark 11:26

57

The lure of pornography

Sex is everywhere, television, internet, magazine, and films. We know that sex is good and reserved for marriage. However, if we can get their eyes off the creator and drop the seed of pornography into their spirit, we now have something to work with. Pornography starts with a seed, an image, a film, a clip, a view, that scene is where it all starts. Then we go to work on the thought life. Bombard their thought life was lustful thoughts which they feel they cannot overcome and as pornography is so easily assessable, they will be logging on in no time. Before you know it, men will no longer find pleasure in their wives, women will neglect their husbands, Children will be advanced in things that should not concern them, and ministers will be bound by the grip of lust. This sin is like a web the longer you stay, the more entangled you become, and those soft little cobwebs the person is flirting with will soon become bars of steel in which they feel they cannot escape.

As they become entangled make them feel helpless to its lure on their soul, this helplessness will eventually lead to hopelessness, which pushes the believer away from God believing they cannot escape, they'll never be free, which leads to the spirit of condemnation. Every time they pray, they'll never do it again only to fall foul to its grip once more. If they depend on will power, they will fail every time, but if they depend on the Holy Spirit, they will win every time.

What people fail to see is that the same devil that tempts them into watching porn is the same devil that turns around and condemns them when they have committed the act. Secrecy is king for this sin, the cover of darkness is where we hold them captive, the one held by it cannot speak about it to anyone for fear of being alienated or ridiculed. So, keep them bound by keeping them quiet. This sin has many people bound in churches. Even the preacher that preaches against it in public is sometimes held captive by it in secret. However, if they confess their sin, we can no longer hold them, if they confess and forsake, then their free. So, keep them quite so we can keep them bound.

THE SOLUTION

For this is the will of God, your sanctification: that you abstain from sexual immorality;

1ˢᵗ Thessalonians 4:3

58

Use gossip to destroy the church

Never underestimate the power of an uncontrolled tongue.

We use gossipers and slanderers to go to work in the church; these men and women are our 5th column in the church. Let me explain.

A *fifth column* is any group of people who undermine a larger group—such as a nation or a besieged city—this takes place from within, usually in favor of an enemy group or nation.

The fifth column are the people we use on the inside to destroy our enemy. We use their tongue to destroy their church, the ministry, the pastor and anything good coming from the church. People who gossip are our entry points into the hearts of the people, if we infect them with negative words, we can infect them with a negative mind and it is that simple.

Allow the gossipers to be saved but never allow them to get converted. Many people get saved, but they're minds aren't renewed which means their tongue is still poisonous.

If they ever get converted, they'll begin to talk about Jesus, and we don't want that.

This tool is useful as the spirit of gossip is always accompanied by their best friend 'The Critical Spirit' Gossip and criticisms are powerful keys in destroying any church. When gossip spreads about a ministry people won't go there because of what they have heard.

Words have destroyed Marriages, Homes, Businesses, Ministries and people's lives.

Use gossip to destroy the church.

THE WARNING

A perverse person stirs up conflict,
and a gossip separates close friends.

Proverbs 16:28

59

THE ASSIGNMENT AGAINST:
The praise and worship team

Praise and worship are one of the church's most powerful tools in living in the presence of God, when they are in constant praise, nothing will get to them when they live a life of thanksgiving and worship their lives become impenetrable. God inhabits the praises of his people. So, we must weaken or if possible, destroy the Praise and worship team.

The bigger the praise and worship team the better. Use the works of the flesh to dismantle the team. We use the usual, jealousy, envy, pride and strife to separate, divide and conquer this work better when we use people's words as the darts, which enter the heart and destroy the relationships.

Create power struggles within the praise and worship as well as the other ministries in the church.

All these result in squabbles and fights. What they fail to realise is God cannot work in that type of environment, because where there is envying and strife, there is confusion and every evil work. But we must not let them band together; if they ever come together on one accord, they will win.

If they are anointed to sing, then we are really in trouble. David played and drove out evil spirits if they begin to tap into the power of their praise, we won't be able to get near them.

They must never recognise the power of their praise.

When they are unified, they are unstoppable.

THE SOLUTION

Behold, how good and how pleasant it is for brethren to dwell together in unity! It is like the precious ointment upon the head, that ran down upon the beard, even Aaron's beard: that went down to the skirts of his garments;

Psalms 133:1-2

60

THE ASSIGNMENT AGAINST:
The Prophetic

Prophecy is given of edification, exhortation and comfort anything outside of that can cause harm. So, cause the person with the prophetic gift, to cultivate the gift, but lapse on character. Let them hunger more for the power of God, but refuse to ignore the promptings of the spirit when he desires changes in their character.

Christians are desperate for the power of God, some will fast and pray for hours, they will go to meetings and seminars, cry out for the power of God, some will receive a gift, if they receive a gift, we have a problem, they can use it to encourage, exalt, edify and even win people to Jesus. However, if they possess a spiritual gift without a mature character, we can discredit the work. There are prophetic people who gossip about others, there are people who can tell you your name and address but are cold and bitter, can prophesy the mind of Christ but are deeply rooted in pride.

A person's character flaws will soon taint their ministry. They may possess great gifts but if their character sucks people will use them for their gift but won't stick around for fellowship.

There are men and woman who can heal the sick but will not forgive their spouse. Can perform miracles, but find fault with everyone. Can prophesy accurately but are living immoral lives. Have the gift of discernment but are yet extremely critical

For maximum effect place someone over the prophetic ministry and the intercessory ministry who has an ulterior motive.... their own.

THE SOLUTION

But the one who prophesies speaks to people for their strengthening, encouraging and comfort.

1st Corinthians 14:3

61

Discredit the prophetic

If you cannot manipulate the heart of the prophet, then use the reverse tactic do your best to belittle the prophetic in every way. If the church adheres to the prophetic, we will lose much ground. The prophetic is dangerous, it can pinpoint our plans and strategies, stop our work in families, marriages, nations, and governments. The prophetic can undo years of chaos we have caused in a second and give people direction. So, use every attack possible introduce Balaam, Balaam was hired to curse the Children of Israel, he tried three times to do this but failed, but fortunately, his spirit is still in the earth. These prophets see the church as a cash cow and use their gift to earn as much money as possible. God spoke directly to Balaam but his heart was not right with God, his true desire was promotion and riches. There are true prophets out there, but the Balaam spirit brings a bad name to the whole prophetic movement, so bring the prophetic so much abuse, and controversy people want no part of it

If we can ostracize the prophet, no one will take heed to their message.

The prophetic ministry is a dangerous one as it brings direction to a church and speaks from heaven regarding what they should do. It must be shut down at all cost. This must be done by causing people to disregard the prophetic when it speaks, belittle the message and frown upon the messenger. Bring suspicion to the ministry, because of its strange acts, let it be aired with caution, the prophetic will then begin to feel unwanted and unloved eventually it will diminish and become non-existent in that church, leaving the church without real direction, thus creating a man-made ministry groping in the dark, not knowing which way to go.

THE SOLUTION
Despise not prophesying.

1st Thessalonians 5:20

62
THE ASSIGNMENT AGAINST MARRIAGE:
Adultery

An old favorite which still works today, in fact, I'm so surprised the humans keep falling for it; there is nothing new under the sun in this respect.

The gameplay remains the same, remember nothing just happens, you go to work on the minister, keep him away from their spouse and allow them to form stronger relationships with the opposite sex, these things always start out as friendships, The more time they spend, the easier it will become. When the minister develops a closer relationship with the opposite sex, the obvious will soon take place.

If we want an all-out, separation go to work on the mind. It's easy, inject thoughts that his wife is not as spiritual as she should be, let him see more of her flaws than her good points, this will bring on the notion that he needs a woman more his spiritual equal, instead of being the priest and minister to his wife he will seek a new one.

These thoughts will cause him to justify his adulterous behavior which will cause him to want a divorce.

Minister leaves his wife for another woman. A family destroyed, mission accomplished. But that isn't the only goal.

The goal is the effect on the ministry. It will cause a divide some will side with the adulterous minister, and some will side with innocent wife, the friction will separate the church and a house divided cannot stand, end result is total annihilation of the ministry, even if they continue as a church the ministry will never be as effective as they once were as the stain of sin lingers in the lips on the world.

It will destroy the lives of most young converts; seeing the hypocrisy, they will give up on their Christianity.

This scenario is magnified a thousand times more if the ministry is world renown, its effects on the body of Christ will echo all around the world, my agents in the media will sensationalize the story, if the minister has done it before offer ex-partners money for their stories, and if we really want to spice it up collect stories from disgruntled ex-members who will be willing to tell all on their once beloved pastor. Adultery is the crème de la crème in destroying any Christian and the church because its root bears so many fruits it becomes endless. The story becomes more newsworthy when the minister is caught with the same sex. It doesn't get better than that.

Not to mention the effects it will have on their children, if the act takes place while their children are teenagers this is a perfect weapon to drive that child far from God, adolescence is a delicate age, the devastation of adultery on a ministers child could send them over the edge and away from the presence of God, don't underestimate the power of adultery.

Adultery is still a top ten in discrediting the church.

Use it at all cost.

THE SOLUTION

For this reason a man will leave his father and mother and be united to his wife, and the two will become one flesh

Ephesians 5:31

63

THE ASSIGNMENT AGAINST:
The Teenagers

Make church as dull as possible. No miracles, no signs, and no wonders. When there is no evidence of real Jesus give them my all-out attack. Sex, drugs and money and don't forget fame. Who wants to go to church when you can party? Make the influence of the world as secure as possible. They must have the latest, clothes, phones, gadgets, look, etc.

The church cannot compare to facebook, twitter, snapchat, etc. Nothing has changed, this scheme has just got more technological, but the concept is the same.

Make the youth feel they are missing out. It's easy.

Make the youth service boring, if there is a youth service if there isn't one even better. Continue to bombard them with don't do this, don't do that. We all know humans are going to do what they are not supposed to do.

Don't talk to them about real issues sex, drugs, gangs, their identity, peer pressure, pregnancy, and relationships amongst other things. Let them find out through their friends and the media.

Make it hard for teenagers to talk to church people and easy to open up to sinners, who will give them ungodly advice. For example, they get pregnant, steer them to the person that will tell them "There is nothing wrong with abortion."

Make the ridicule of Christianity unbearable, subject Christian teenagers as much shame as possible, mock them and alienate them and if they put a foot wrong, we'll be waiting for them, "I thought you were supposed to be a Christian?" Will be the line waiting for them.

Only strong Christian teenagers can withstand our onslaught as the pull of the world is almost irresistible.

THE SOLUTION

Remember your Creator in the days of your youth, before the days of trouble come and the years approach when you will say, "I find no pleasure in them."

Ecclesiastes 12:1

64

THE ASSIGNMENT AGAINST THEIR FINANCES
Keep them broke

Don't let Pastor preach on prosperity, keep the people poor by never letting them know their rights to prosperity as a Christian. Money is one of the most dangerous weapons against our kingdom on the earth. Keep them broke by never speaking about giving.

If they sow, they will reap, deter them from sowing. Drive a fear of man into the preacher to never speak about money or giving, because he does not want to be labeled a preacher who is always after your money. So, because of the fear of man cause him to sidestep the issue. We must, by all means, keep the church broke. If the Christian ever gets hold of real money we are in trouble. They can affect the world, if they indeed become prosperous they'll begin to own land and property, television stations, and newspapers, they will affect governments and all kinds of powerful positions, worst still they will empower other people.

THE COUNTER ATTACK

Give, and it will be given to you. A good measure, pressed down, shaken together and running over, will be poured into your lap. For with the measure you use, it will be measured to you.

Luke 6:38

65

Keep them from tithing and giving

Push the ideology that tithing is the Law, (although it came before the law). If they begin to tithe and claim their inheritance according to the word, we're in trouble. The tithe is their protection against our plans, there are too many promises attached to tithing for us not to attack the message. So, begin to sow suspicion of where the money is going, what is the tithe being used for? How much is the pastor being paid? If you can sow doubt among people, they will be reluctant to give. When people focus on these things, they have taken their eyes off his scriptural command and keep the church financially unstable. If they keep the tithe in their pocket, the church is crippled and cannot move forward. They also create holes in their own pocket leaving themselves worse off and open to financial attack.

THE SOLUTION

Bring you all the tithes into the storehouse, that there may be meat in my house, and prove me now herewith, said the LORD of hosts, if I will not open you the windows of heaven, and pour you out a blessing, that there shall not be room enough to receive it.

Malachi 3:10

66

Give them a stingy spirit

If the people are stingy, they will never prosper and they'll keep their ministry and themselves in poverty. So cause them to hoard and keep hold of everything. When they lack the knowledge that it is more blessed to give than to receive, they will never be blessed, forgetting that whatever a man sows, that is what he will reap. So if they give a little, they will receive a little. If they are mean and tight-fisted, they will never see the blessing God intended for them, and they will rarely enjoy what they have.

THE WARNING
But this I say, He who sows sparingly shall reap also sparingly; and he who sows bountifully shall reap also bountifully.

2 Corinthians 9:6

67

THE ASSIGNMENT AGAINST EVANGELISM:
Discourage evangelism

Jesus last words were that they would be a witness unto him throughout the uttermost parts of the earth, but today some churches put little enthuses on evangelism. So promote a belief that evangelism is so last century, it infringes on people's beliefs. Cloud them with the ideat hat they are forcing their views on others.

Terrify them into sharing their faith one to one, scared as to what people might think about them.

Make standing on a street corner talking about Jesus look embarrassing and push the notion that it is not to be done like that anymore. It's offensive and imposes on people's civil rights. Not knowing this is what each believer was called to do, be a witness.

If they do not witness people won't hear the message, if people don't hear the message, people won't believe.

The preaching of the gospel is the power of God unto salvation, no gospel, no power, so keep them scared and keep them quiet.

So, discourage evangelism, instead offer the sinner's tea and movies (that have nothing to do with Jesus) it is more civilized. What they will fail to realize is this civilized approach is winning no one to Christ and brings no conviction on sin.

THE SOLUTION

And he said unto them, Go ye into all the world, and preach the gospel to every creature.

Mark 16:15

68
THE ASSIGNMENT AGAINST:
The pastor's wife

If you can't get the pastor then go to work on the wife, Due to the busy schedule of her husband (if they don't have an understanding of each other's call) we can make the wife feel neglected, unworthy, insignificant and incapable. This will result in low self-esteem; she'll put on a pleasant smile and a lovely dress, but inside she'll be dying inside.

Make her feel inferior, insignificant and unqualified to stand next to her husband, invade her mind with thoughts that she does not pray enough, fast enough, visit the sick, speak in tongues, etc. Enough condemnation will cause her to want to give up or drive her into depression and condemnation. There is nothing new under the sun. As it was in the beginning, the way to the man is the woman, when you can get to the woman, this will lead to disruption in the home and when a man's home isn't right his life won't be right. Stress at home will eventually affect the pulpit, he'll eventually crack, and family will break (if they're not strong) we can cause a broken home, mission accomplished.

If the husband becomes so pre-occupied, he does not notice her demise, the continued work on her mind will cause her to give up.

The mind is the battleground, that's where we work

If the pastor neglects his wife enough, she will feel unloved and begin to look for love elsewhere or she will start to believe the neglect means her husband is seeing someone else, provoking jealousy and mistrust in the relationship, resulting in more strife. Since trust is the backbone of any relationship when that is gone, we continue the bombardment on the mind, driving a wedge in their relationship, even if he is innocent.

So, attack the wife, attack her mind with suggestions if she does not renew her mind sooner or later, it will be the beginning of the end.

The attack on the wife is paramount. To get to Adam, we needed Eve.

THE WARNING
Can two walk together, except they be agreed?

Amos 3:3

69

THE ASSIGNMENT AGAINST:
The Pastor

Attack the head, in the natural if you severe the hand or the foot there a strong possibility you'll live, but if you aim for the head there's an even stronger possibility you'll die, the attack on the pastor is paramount.

    The next few pages deal with the leader. The shepherd is the one holding everything together so the attack must be strategic, ongoing and relentless. If he is not praying, studying his word and seeking God, he's open to attack. If we can take out the Pastor, we've succeeded. The next few pages deals with the takedown of the pastor.

70

Work the Pastor to death

A pastor's job is demanding, so we turn up the heat and keep them constantly busy. When the pastor does not take a day off, when he has no break in the routine, takes no holiday, always busy all these are the elements on the pathway to burnout.

The demands of pastoring are a path which, if not careful can wear him out. This pastor knows nothing about delegation.

Again, the issues are similar to the failure to take a day off. Work, work, work, work, if God rested after 6 days why are many trying to outdo him? Give the pastor a fear that if he takes a break or rests from their duty that the church will fall apart without them. If it does that it means the church was built around the man and not on God.

THE SOLUTION

Come to me, all who labor and are heavy laden, and I will give you rest. Take my yoke upon you, and learn from me, for I am gentle and lowly in heart, and you will find rest for your souls. For my yoke is easy, and my burden is light.

Matthew 11:28-30

71

The leader that will listen to no one

This person is so spiritual no one is on their level, no one can talk to them, and no one can advise them of an issue in their life, ministry, marriage or family. When a minister has this mindset, the results will be catastrophic. It's an accident waiting to happen.

As great as Moses was, he needed Jethro's advice, the great Samuel needed Eli, and the disciples needed one another, but this leader fails to realize any of this and believes s/he can make it on their own. No one can talk to this minister, and this minister usually rejects the very thing sent to help them.

No one can talk to this person; I mean no one, wife/husband, friends, family, not even God. This leader doesn't listen to anybody, what this leader does not realize they are setting up themselves for a fall and a collapse is inevitable. This leader thinks they know it all, and when people think they know it all they will usually cease from gaining more knowledge, a leader must be a continuous learner, but not this person. Pastors who fail to learn continuously are not nearly as wise as those who do. Again, this disposition can lead to a fall, and when this type of leader falls, everybody else falls with them.

THE WARNING
But the king interrupted him and said, "Since when have I made you the king's counselor? Be quiet now before I have you killed!"
So the prophet stopped with this warning:
"I know that God has determined to destroy you because you have done this and have refused to accept my counsel."

2 Chronicles 25:16

72

Physical exercise must be alien to the leader

The pastor must not get fit or look after their health, let them stay up late, get little sleep, eat late, put on weight and never go to the doctors. Let them preach divine healing but never understand divine health. The pastor is usually selfless, so he will forget about himself, focus on everybody else and often remain that way until his body sends some sort of warning signal that something is wrong. By that time the damage would have already started. Cancer, high blood pressure, heart disease, diabetes, high cholesterol you name it, all these can be avoided with a healthy lifestyle so deter the pastor from getting fit.

THE COUNTER ATTACK

Physical training is good, but training for godliness is much better, promising benefits in this life and in the life to come.

1st Timothy 4:8

73

Get the Pastor angry...Continually

No one wants to serve under an angry pastor

Get the Pastor angry, but it must be an unholy anger, if they are angry with sin they will preach with passion and influence men. However, if they are mad with their spouse, children or people, they will use the platform to vent their anger, which will usually do more harm than good. Anger is the terminal illness for preachers. Anger that is allowed to simmer and stew for any length of time will kill a ministry, if not the minister. Angry words kill both the speaker and the listener. It does far more damage than good. Pastors will not accomplish a fraction of what they think they will achieve if they vent their anger on the people.

Angry Pastors hurt people and the damage is far worse when it comes from the pastors.

Angry Pastors Have Control Issues

Angry Pastors Lose Top Staff – Quality staff leave churches with angry pastors. Life is too short, and they have other options. So even if a culture is healthy, they self-destruct it because they cannot function where there is peace.

Angry Pastors Become Merely Positional Leaders – If a pastor proclaims, "I am the pastor," he/she is no longer the leader. If a leader has to tell you they're the leader, they are not. They are now leading by position rather than influence.

Angry Pastors Do Lasting Harm to Churches – Every church led by an angry pastor will decline in attendance and rarely returned to its previous level of impact because no congregation member in their right mind wants to give up their Sunday mornings to be abused.

Angry Pastors Lack Self-Awareness – They have a perverted sense of being right, and everyone else is wrong.

ANGRY PASTORS ARE A TOOL WE USE FOR OFFENDING OTHERS

THE COUNTER ATTACK
Know this, my beloved brothers: let every person be quick to hear, slow to speak, slow to anger;

James 1:19

74

Burnout the pastor

Bombard him with things to do, have everyone call him and everyone wanting something, pull him left right and centre. If they has a soft heart, s/he will find it hard to say no to people, so they will try to help everybody on the way to killing themselves.

Give the pastor no help, and place people around them that only take, take, take. If they fails to realize what they are doing to themselves, they will be sick in no time.

Usually, in this circumstance, only a few people will really help the leader, but if the leader fails to listen, soon the church will eventually have to find them a new Pastor. Repeat the process.

Burn out is on the increase. Leaders have a passion for changing the world and thinking they can do so by themselves. So, allow the leader to change the world on the way to burn out and use their congregation to help them.

THE SOLUTION

And He said to them, "Come with me privately to a solitary place, and let us rest for a while." For many people were coming and going, and they did not even have time to eat.

Mark 6:31

75

Discouragement through ungratefulness

Let me explain, Ministers, help people all the time; it's in the job description. They can't help themselves. They will clothe the naked, help the homeless, give money to the needy, people come looking for help, and they support them. People get saved, the minister pours out and builds them up, he or she may help them financially, get them a job and help them through college. Aid them through their family problems, get their kids out of jail and go above and beyond the call of service because they have the heart to do so. There are some people that minister gives their all for, as they just desire to do good or they recognize the gift in that person and genuinely want to see others succeed.

We then bring in sharp division (usually through people) and separate them. When people who ministers have poured their time and teaching into turn their back on their beloved mentor it causes major league discouragement. These leaders are left feeling they have wasted their time and energy with someone who is ungrateful. Most pastors forget that they should do everything as onto their Lord, but who remembers this when they are facing discouragement.

This weapon of discouragement is valuable against any mentor. It breaks their heart and brings a wounded spirit and entry point for us to work through.

Discouragement through ungratefulness.

THE SOLUTION

Whatever you do, work heartily, as for the Lord and not for men, knowing that from the Lord you will receive the inheritance as your reward. You are serving the Lord Christ.

Colossians 3:23-4

76

Create a man-centered leadership

Cause the church to be centered on one man...not Jesus, but the pastor. Let it be one man's vision, one man's dream, he can build it as big as he wants but don't let him rise up a successor.

It is no longer about equipping the saints for the work of the ministry but people coming to hear what I have to say and doing what I tell them.

The next generation is not important to this pastor, but only what they can accomplish. This pastor has forgotten a leader's job is to raise up other leaders, so now you have frustrated people in the church who know they have been called by God to do great work but don't know how to accomplish it.

If we can stop anyone from succeeding the visionary, we have killed the work. Success is nothing without a successor.

THE SOLUTION

And the LORD said unto Moses, Take you Joshua the son of Nun, a man in whom is the spirit, and lay your hand upon him;

Numbers 27:18

77

Deter the Pastor from preaching the return of Christ

If they don't hear they won't know and they won't prepare. So, cause the preacher to sidestep the return of Christ. Let them get so caught up in the now they forget the Lord is at. When people aren't informed, the will not be prepared. They won't look out for the signs, ignore the news, and they will not realize the importance of the preaching the gospel.

Soon they will forget they are sojourners and pilgrims and overlook the fact that this world is not theirs and become preoccupied with the here and now. The focus on their preaching is now, what they can get, who they can become and how successful they can be. While all these teachings are good, if they forget the real reason for their salvation, they will lose focus on what they are really supposed to do.

THE COUNTER ATTACK

Let your moderation be known to all men. The Lord is at hand.

Philippians 4:5

78

The Minister must not spend time with God

Keep the Minster busy at all cost; when the ministers are busy it will cloud their judgment, their views, and their discernment. Under no circumstances must they spend quality time with God. When their discernment is clouded, you can bring people alongside them whose character is unsavory who are doing things they should not do with people they should not be doing them with and their exposure will affect the ministry. When they do not spend time with God, they will make silly mistakes, judge by what they see and believe everything they hear, so keep them away from God's presence.

If the minister spends time with God, they will hear from heaven and receive instruction which will destroy our work.

THE SOLUTION

but they who wait for the LORD shall renew their strength; they shall mount up with wings like eagles; they shall run and not be weary; they shall walk and not faint.

Isaiah 40:31

79

Promote rebellion towards leadership

This is done when people highlight more what the leader is doing wrong than what they do right. When the leaders failings are in the spotlight, their leadership qualities are now called into question. Those that doubt your capability to lead will soon rebel against your commandments to go forward.

Rebellion is conceived in the heart and breathed out in conversation, so pinpoint the person most likely to be used to rebel against the God-ordained authority.

Always remember the reason for their rebellion must be because 'God told me to". (It makes it more believable).

This type of rebellion is achieved through those closes to the leader. You go to work on those closes to leadership, when they rebel against the leadership it will cause the most pain. When people hurt the leader, that leader will have little or no trust in future protégés.

THE SOLUTION

Now we exhort you, brothers, warn them that are unruly, comfort the feebleminded, support the weak, be patient toward all men.

1 Thessalonians 5:14

80

Go to work on the flaw in the man or woman of God

Use the flaw in the Minister to cause them to fall. Whether it be anger, pride, loneliness, rejection, whatever their flaw is in their character, work on their weakness to destroy them. What most people don't realize is the flaw in their life is sometimes allowed to stay there to keep them entirely dependent upon God, but keep them ignorant of this fact.

THE SOLUTION

But He said to me, "My grace is sufficient for you, for My power is perfected in weakness." Therefore I will boast all the more gladly in my weaknesses, so that the power of Christ may rest on me.

2 Corinthians 12:9

81

Give the Minister a problem so embarrassing he cannot bring it to anyone

Problems will arise, but cause a problem so big to emerge in the life of the minister; he cannot share it with anybody. This is the problem they sweep under the carpet but comes back to trip them up later on in life.

Make it so embarrassing (in their mind's eye) that they cannot bring it to anybody as they will become afraid of what people may think of them. Make it so daunting they cannot confide in anyone.

Be it a health problem, a ministry problem, sex problem, a dark secret from the past, anything which their mind believes they cannot share with someone, keep them bound, by keeping them quiet.

As his or her ministry grows so too will the problem, but it's an area shut up and closed.

The frustration of having that area of their life shut out with no outlet for help will create a fear of being found out, resulting in preachers setting others free but yet they themselves still remaining bound.

We do this by placing people around the leader they cannot trust or confide in and in the fullness of time their fears will begin to control them, and as fear works in the reverse of faith sooner or later, it will be exposed.

THE COUNTER ATTACK

He that covers his sins shall not prosper: but whosoever confesses and forsakes them shall have mercy.

Proverbs 28:13

82

Let the Minister save everyone else's family except their own

This sometimes happens without them even knowing, they concentrate so hard on everyone else, they lose track of what is going on in their own home. Their ministry is growing; finances are increasing, new ventures and programs but often at the expense of their own family. Therefore, give them a heart to evangelise the world but forget about their own children, provide them with a heart for the gospel but at the expense of their family.

If they don't spend time with their children, speak to them and encourage them, someone else will, that is where we come in. We give their children everything they were missing, Sex, Drugs and Rock and Roll (or Hip Hop, whatever takes their fancy). Let the minister miss out on the years that their child was growing up. By the time the minister realises his neglect, it will be too late, and you cannot gain back wasted years. This also causes pain and regret for the minister which if their faith is not strong will result in heartache.

Let the minister save everyone else's family except their own.

THE SOLUTION

And if it seem evil unto you to serve the LORD, choose you this day whom you will serve; whether the gods which your fathers served that were on the other side of the River, or the gods of the Amorites, in whose land you dwell: but as for me and my house, we will serve the LORD.

Joshua 24:15

83

Influence the Pastor to build without God

Get the pastor to build the ministry, but without God, How? Influence him to build on great ideas, but not on revelation knowledge, Great ideas are good, but revelation knowledge is deadly. If the leader gets a revelation of God's will for the church nothing can stop them. We must keep them from obtaining revelation at any cost.

So, promote head knowledge over revealed knowledge, head knowledge is easy to access and mentally worked out. Revealed knowledge comes from God and takes time to access, but effective when applied.

So, give him great ideas, other people's input, suggestions, and comments.

Let them attend conferences on church growth, church building, thinking if it worked for them it will work for me, this type of behaviour creates a 'let's do what that church is doing mentality', This thought pattern creates a carbon copy church, never allowing them to find God's will for their ministry, thus causing them not to fulfil God's will for their life.

Cause the leader to do everything without God; the church will never be able to stand the storm if it's built by a man

Get him to rely on others and not on God. This is easy, in a microwave style Christianity and fingertip technology, and Google as our friend, nobody wants to spend time in prayer anymore. Motivate them to build without God.

THE SOLUTION

*I am the vine, you are the branches: He that abides in me,
and I in him, the same brings forth much fruit:
for without me you can do nothing.*

John 15:5

84

Give the Pastor a desire to be famous

This hunger for fame is an old age favorite. Let the real motive be the lust for power and prestige. If this is the minister's real desire, he will manipulate people, do what God did not tell him to do, go where God did not send him, work with people God did not want him to work with and operate ahead of his timing. All because of a strong desire for fame and fortune. Give people a passion for a megachurch even if God has not called them to be a pastor, blind the hearts of people going into ministry that they only see the glamour and not the pain.

Now it becomes about quantity and not quality. This will ultimately lead to the ministry being less about Jesus and more about the Man, so now they are promoting the pastor and not the cross, if not careful this will soon result in Pride (see Pride) which will then cause them to be a law unto themselves, they will eventually refuse council or correction, help or direction from anyone. Anyone who appears to oppose them is deemed rebellious when really, they are trying to help. By this time the minister is in self-destruction mode. This will result in a fear factor for those around them which will bring a snare to the ministry.

THE WARNING

For they loved the glory that comes from man more than the glory that comes from God.

John 12:43

85

Discredit the leader

In any Battle/War, if you can attack the head, you've won. The attack on the leadership is paramount to our war against the church. Find any story necessary whether they are true or false, old or new, who cares if it happened twenty years ago, people will tarnish people with the sins of their past. People love to hear negative stories.

Many Christians themselves do not realise this and are usually the same pawns we use to bring down one another.

The most successful attacks which cause the most havoc come from within.

So, create stories about their marriage if they are married, their single life if they are single. Find a story and magnify its negatives qualities. If you smite the shepherd, the sheep shall scatter.

Then, discredit the leader. When this is done we have executed our duty, no one wants to listen to a leader they do not trust.

THE WARNING

"Strike the Shepherd that the sheep may be scattered; And I will turn My hand against the little ones.

Zechariah 13:7

86

Money must be the new motivation of the preacher and not the Gospel

Many preachers start off humble, but as they begin to be used by God and God starts to exalt them a new goal often enters the arena, the love of money. Now it becomes less about the gospel and more about what they can get. Therefore, we lavish the preacher with gifts; we use the gifts to manipulate the preacher. If they are not focused the gifts will begin to affect the heart.

Many forget why they entered the ministry and money becomes the new motivation. There are some who are stronger than others who are able to stay committed to God without being a slave to mammon, but those ministers with the lust in their heart for money, these are the ones we can go to work on, and if they allow the gifts to pervert the heart then we have them.

Now when the love of money is in operation the altar call for souls is no longer heard, but the call for offerings and seeds go without saying.

This spirit will also be a strong factor that will cause many preachers to miss God, Why? Now the minister will only accept invites from churches with a large congregation or who can afford the price, but ignore the promptings of the Holy Spirit when directed to a church that appears to be below their expected income bracket

THE WARNING
For the love of money is a root of all sorts of evil, and some by longing for it have wandered away from the faith and pierced themselves with many grief's.

1st Timothy 6:10

87

The ministry team

Place people around the leader that will only tell him what he wants to hear. They dare not speak against anything the leader says, that way if the leader ever makes a wrong decision he will never know because no one dares tell him and if someone does try to correct them this leader will never comply, listen or believe the person trying to bring the correction. In fact, if anybody does try to correct the leader, this leader will think the one who is trying to correct them is trying to oppose them is of the devil trying to destroy them when really that person is there to help them.

THE SOLUTION
A servant of the Lord must not quarrel but must be kind to everyone, be able to teach, and be patient with difficult people.

2nd Timothy 2:24

88

The Leader must never recognise those sent into their life to aid them in their life assignment

This is a familiar scenario. Often Leaders fail to recognise the people sent into their life to help them. Often God will send different kinds of people with various gifts to elevate the ministry to another level, whether it be media, music, the prophetic, etc. These men and women are sent into the ministry with gifts the leader does not possess to help in the areas the leader knows nothing about. These people sent will be different, some may have character flaws, personality traits which the church is not familiar with but nevertheless, they have been sent to help the ministry, with help in time and with training the person sent can become the person God has called them to be. But if all the leader sees is a person's flaws it will cause the leader to reject the very thing sent to help them.

Leaving the ministry struggling in the area where they need help the most.

THE WARNING

While he was still speaking, the king said to him,
"Have we appointed you an adviser to the king? Stop!
Why be struck down?" So the prophet stopped but said,
"I know that God has determined to destroy you, because you have done this and have not listened to my counsel.

2 Chronicles 25:16

89

Whatever you do, don't let them…..Pray

Do everything in your power to hinder them from praying, create longer work hours, introduce more sporting activities, hold major events on Sundays, cause them to tell their problems to their friends, their parents, their counsellor or psychiatrist but don't let them tell God, give them a desire for entertainment, but don't let them discover the benefits of prayer.

Do everything in your power to stop the Christian praying. Prayer releases the will of God into their lives, Prayer hinders us from working the way we want to work, and prayer brings God into their lives, circumstances, and situations. When they open their mouth, they can have whatsoever they ask, and if they pray according to his will, he will do it. Prayer is the Christians open invitation to gain everything God has to offer; he told them ask of me the Nations. He told them Ask, Seek, Knock and if they persistently pray, they will get what they have been asking for.

Discourage them from praying to make them feel that nothing is happening, what is the point? God is not answering; try to cause them to seek their own way.

If we fail to distract, derail or hinder them from praying, we will be weakened considerably in our efforts to plunge the world into darkness. If they call upon him, he will answer them and show them mighty things they do not know.

If the Christian finds out their authority in prayer and uses it, this will jeopardize all our endeavors to plunge the world into darkness.

Many know the power of prayer, they recognize its benefits, and know it works but are not willing to pay the price; the price of prayer is TIME.

Fill their time with everything else, family time, friends, relatives, over time, steal their time, take up their time, cause them to never make time and we have succeeded in our endeavors. The television was the greatest invention of the twentieth century along with the advent of the internet, phones, now we have social media use these things to keep them from praying use this and every conceivable gadget known to entertain man. When used effectively these items create the greatest distraction to prayer ever known. Whatever you do don't let them Pray.

If they add Fasting to their prayer, it now steps up a gear, and they can be deadly to the kingdom of darkness.

If they fast for the right reasons, with the right motives, this act will paralyze our activities

      Stop them praying at all cost.

THE COUNTER ATTACK

The effectual fervent prayer of a righteous man availeth much.

James 5:16

90

Whatever you do, don't let them…..
Seek for the Baptism of the Holy Spirit

If they get this everything we have worked for will come crashing down around us, if ministers, church members, boys, and girls hit the power line of heaven we are really in trouble.

We have convinced many that these things are passed and were only for 1st-century believers, but there are many who know the truth and will stop at nothing to receive the power from on high.

Christians receive the Spirit upon their conversion. This means that they are saved most are happy with this, they're going to heaven, and that's all they need to do. The secondary" experience is the baptism of the Holy Spirit

If they get this, they will be effective, they will preach differently, speak different, act different, they'll even start to look different. The baptism of the Holy Ghost is the most powerful weapon in the Christian artillery, and many do not believe in this experience. Many still believe you have to work for it; many do not cultivate their relationship enough to press in for more.

So we must push to make them feel unworthy, unloved and not good enough to receive the gift. Condemnation has and will always be our all-time favorite in the war on the mind.

So go to work on the mind. Hinder them from becoming desperate enough to seek this experience. This experience will gain them spiritual power, a holy boldness, empowerment for service and the ability to live a victorious Christian life despite what we throw at them, they'll speak in a language we cannot intercept and begin to get more profound revelations of the things of God. This is why it is imperative we keep them from seeking this gift. They will expel demons, heal the sick, raise the dead and do miracles this world has never known if they succeed in their quest for this gift, we must ensure it does not take place. If it does, it will be to our detriment.

THE SOLUTION

But you will receive power when the Holy Spirit comes upon you, and you will be My witnesses in Jerusalem, and in all Judea and Samaria, and to the ends of the earth."

Acts 1:8

91

Whatever you do, don't let them….. Build Up their faith

If we can stop them believing (for anything) we've won, their belief in what they have been asking for is also another powerful weapon of the Christian. It has stated so many times in their Bible if they can just believe, all things are possible to them that believe, so destroy their faith; we do this by throwing every conceivable dart at the Christian. Delay, postpone and fight to keep their blessing from them. Weaken their faith by causing them to doubt and disbelieve God's word. Assign people around them that feed their doubts. If they hear faith they'll be filled with faith, if they hear doubt, they'll weaken. So hinder them from hearing faith-filled words.

But whatever you do don't let them build up their faith.

Their faith can move mountains, heal and deliver and more importantly their faith is what pleases God, so attack their faith in every conceivable way. Use everything in this handbook to destroy their faith.

THE SOLUTION
But without faith, it is impossible to please him

Hebrews 11:6

92

OUR NUMBER ONE AIM: THE SINNER MUST NEVER GET SAVED

With all we have discussed, the church is the vehicle which proclaims the Gospel in which men are saved. Every strategy used culminates into this last point. We must stop people from receiving Christ. They must never be ready, let them think they have to earn salvation, keep them blinded by every distraction and let them never come to the knowledge of the truth.

We use every possible trick in the book to deter the sinner from making the decision to follow Jesus.

Make them think they have lots of time, enjoy their life, suggest there any many ways to heaven, all you have to be is a good person; God loves everybody, Jesus was a good guy, etc.

Bring in every conceivable lie necessary to deter them from making that step to receiving Christ, keep the blindfold over their minds.

If they receive him, we would have lost the battle. They would of escaped hell and now have peace with God through his son. They will enjoy fellowship with God, peace, joy, and intimacy and at the end, an eternity in Heaven.

THE SOLUTION

That if thou shalt confess with thy mouth the Lord Jesus, and shalt believe in thine heart that God hath raised him from the dead, thou shalt be saved.

Romans 10:9

Want to know God?

It all starts with accepting Jesus Christ as your Lord and Savior. Jesus Christ provides a relationship with the Father and eternal life through His death on the cross and resurrection.

Romans 10:9 promises, "If you confess with your mouth Jesus as Lord, and believe in your heart that God raised Him from the dead, you will be saved." If you have not yet begun your personal relationship with God, understand that God loves you with an everlasting love, it does not matter what you have done or how far you have gone away from him, he is waiting to receive you.

If you are willing to take this step to follow Jesus. You can tell Him in your own words or use this simple prayer:

Lord Jesus, I ask you to forgive my sins and save me from eternal separation from God. By faith, I accept your work and death on the cross as sufficient payment for my sins. Thank You for providing the way for me to know you and to have a relationship with my heavenly Father. Through faith in You, I have eternal life. Thank You also for hearing my prayers and loving me unconditionally. Please give me the strength, wisdom, and determination to walk in the centre of your will. In Jesus' name, Amen.

If you have just prayed this prayer, congratulations!

You have received Christ as your Savior and have made the best decision you will ever make, you are now a new creature *(2 Corinth 5; 17)*, and all your sins are forgiven.

Now, get yourself a Bible, find a good bible believing church and draw close to God. You have just begun a brand-new exciting life with Christ Jesus, and he will finish the work he started in you *Philippians 1:6*

If you have made this decision, please email me and let me know so I can rejoice with you and help you in any way possible

info@decisionsdeterminedestiny.com

THE POWER OF WORDS

The WINNER'S MENTALITY

★ ★ ★ ★ ★

- ▶ Discover how to hold your tongue in the most trying times.
- ▶ Discover the real power you posses with the words you speak.
- ▶ Discover how what you say has a profound effect on your life.
- ▶ Discover how your life will begin to consist of the things you confess.

THE POWER OF WORDS:

The Winners Mentality consists of 21 Chapters regarding, the use, effects, benefits and consequences of the words which we speak and the influence they have on our lives and the lives of those around us.

ISBN: 9781909425781

🅣 winnermentality 📷 winnersmentality

ORDER YOUR COPY TODAY.
WWW.KEVINTREASURE.COM

Kevin A. Treasure

DECISIONS DETERMINE DESTINY:

Stories and Scenarios

The Decisions You Make Today, Determine Where You'll Be Tomorrow

www.DecisionsDetermineDestiny.com

www.ingramcontent.com/pod-product-compliance
Lightning Source LLC
Chambersburg PA
CBHW070430010526
44118CB00014B/1985